Other titles in the Successful Strategist series:

The Learning Organization, Bob Garratt
Cultures and Organizations, Geert Hofstede

Titles in the Successful Manager series:

The Successful Manager's Guide to Europe, Kevin Featherstone
Managing Your Own Career, Dave Francis
Learning to Lead, Bob Garratt
Manage Your Time, Sally Garratt
Superteams, Colin Hastings, Peter Bixby, Rani Chaudhry-Lawton
Managing Yourself, Mike Pedler and Tom Boydell
Finance for the Perplexed Executive, Ray Proctor
Action Learning, Krystyna Weinstein
Managing People, Vivien Whitaker

MAX BOISOT

Information and Organizations

The Manager as Anthropologist

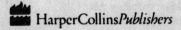 HarperCollins*Publishers*

HarperCollins*Publishers*
77–85 Fulham Palace Road,
Hammersmith, London W6 8JB

This paperback edition 1994
9 8 7 6 5 4 3 2 1

Previously published in paperback by Fontana 1987

ISBN 0 00 637126 4

Set in Linotron Palatino by
Rowland Phototypesetting Ltd
Bury St Edmunds, Suffolk

Printed in Great Britain by
HarperCollinsManufacturing Glasgow

To the most astute anthropologists of them all, my daughters, Saskia and Abigail, in the hope that they never decide to publish their family field notes.

Acknowledgements

The key concepts developed in this book first emerged from research work that I carried out as Research Associate at the Euro-Asia Centre (EAC) at INSEAD and I would like to thank Henri-Claude de Bettignies, the EAC's founder and guiding light for his support.

Also at various times, my thinking has greatly benefited from discussions with Gordon Redding, John Child, Manfred Mack, Carlo Brumat, and tirelessly with Bob Garratt the series editor. Without trying to offload a responsibility that as author is mine alone to bear, I thank them all.

Contents

Introduction 11

PART ONE · CONCEPTS

1 The Structuring of Information 25
2 Information Sharing 42
3 Codification-Diffusion: C-D Theory 59
4 Knowledge Cycles 77
5 Transactional Strategies 94

PART TWO · APPLICATIONS

6 The Industrial Enterprise in the C-Space 113
7 Technology 133
8 The Evolution of the Firm in the C-Space 152
9 The Firm's External Relations in the C-Space 169
10 The Multinational Firm in the C-Space 185
11 Corporate Culture in the C-Space 202
12 Managing in the People's Republic of China 218
13 Conclusions 234

Index 247

Introduction

The Challenge of Complexity

It is a commonplace to say that the manager's job is characterized by increasing complexity. Whatever the size of the firm he happens to work in, he is required to operate in a wider and more integrated environment than ever before. And within it, signals travel incomparably faster and more densely than they used to, foreshadowing a far larger class of events that must be interpreted and responded to than hitherto. As the French historian, Fernand Braudel, has shown, two hundred years ago a letter sent from London would take two weeks to reach Venice. Today the contents of that letter can be transmitted electronically in less than one second.[1]

Faced with complexity, the traditional instinct of the practical manager has been to try to reduce it through the use of rules of thumb, standard operating procedures, etc. If this did not always succeed in eliminating uncertainty, it certainly helped to reduce anxiety, allowing life to go on at a lower level of neurosis than otherwise.

Yet reducing complexity is only an option if some measure of insight and understanding are present, if, through the myriad stimuli that rain upon him at each instant, the manager can discern some minimum structure that can help him make sense of his situation. Failing this, complexity can only be absorbed and endured. And while most people vary in their willingness and ability to deal with complexity – this is very much a matter of personality and cognitive style – few of them other than mystics or simpletons can live with it for long when it operates at very high levels.

Complexity is first and foremost a challenge to our individual data processing powers. Where complexity cannot be reduced, or where we as individuals are unwilling or unable to absorb it, these data processing powers must somehow be expanded. This is one purpose of organization: to harness the data processing potential of a group of individuals where task complexity proves too much for any one of them.

Yet as a way of dealing with complexity, organizations confront us with a paradox. For individual data processors can only be said to be organized when they are in some kind of communicative relationship with each other *and such a relationship already presupposes a measure of complexity reduction for messages to be intelligible*. There would thus seem to be a limit to the complexity of what can be collectively shared through oral or written transmission. In such circumstances it can only be the collective *experiencing* of complexity that will give rise to a common understanding of it and such an understanding will often have to be wordless.

Striking an appropriate balance between what can be understood and what can be shared or, more technically, between processing and communicating data, is essentially a *cultural* problem. In their classic 1952 paper on the subject of culture, after reviewing more than three hundred definitions of the term, two cultural anthropologists, Alfred Kroeber and Clyde Kluckhohn, took the term to mean 'patterns, explicit and implicit, of and for behaviour acquired and transmitted by symbols, constituting the distinctive achievements of human groups, including their embodiments in artifacts; the essential core of culture consists of traditional (i.e. historically derived and selected) ideas and especially their attached values; culture systems may, on the one hand, be considered a product of action, on the other as conditioning elements of further action'.[2]

Culture, then, is about the structuring and sharing of information between individuals and groups of varying sizes. To the extent that cultures are considered devices for coping with complexity, they become legitimate objects of study for managers also faced with complexity. In short, to be effective in an ever more complex world, the manager must become something of an anthropologist; hence the subtitle of this book.

Information as Wealth

The information revolution that has been unfolding over the last thirty years or so has massively increased our capacity to structure and to share data, yet the phenomenon is not framed as a *cultural* event. It is perceived as being first and foremost technological in nature. Yet, if, as it is frequently argued today, information must be considered a new form of wealth, does it not follow that culture, taken as the production and exchange of socially relevant information, is a key generator of wealth along with physical resources? Indeed, do not countries like Japan, Singapore, or Hong Kong owe their success primarily to cultural factors rather than to their access to natural resources?

In spite of the incalculable impact that the information revolution is having on our lives and our cultures, we still do not really understand this new form of wealth. We lack what might be called a political economy of information. As Peter Drucker points out in his book *Post-Capitalist Society*,

'We need an economic theory that puts knowledge into the center of the wealth-producing process. Such a theory alone can explain the present economy. It alone can explain economic growth. It alone can explain innovation. It alone can explain how the Japanese economy works and, above all, why it works. It alone can explain why newcomers, especially in high-tech fields, can, almost overnight, sweep the market and drive out all competitors, no matter how well entrenched they are – as the Japanese did in consumer electronics and in the US automobile market.'[3]

A useful first step in any attempt to create a political economy of information would be to follow the advice of Daniel Bell and to see what happens if we decide to treat information as a factor of production. The idea, by itself, is not particularly startling. Social conceptions of wealth have always been associated with the factors critical to production in a given society. In the agrarian economy of Ricardo's day, for example, the critical factors of production were taken to be land and labour. Seventy years later, with the industrial revolution in full swing, the critical factors were labour and capital – the latter being interpreted as the capacity to buy machinery and equipment.

The way that factors of production were combined depended upon the technologies available. The different combinations on offer could be represented by what economists call a *production function*. A production function in which capital and labour are taken as factors of production is shown in Figure 1. The curve A A' indicates the different mixes of capital and labour that can produce a given level of output. Close to point A, capital-intensive technologies will be used; close to point A' labour-intensive technologies will be chosen. Technological progress cannot be explicitly represented in such a diagram; the depiction is a static one representing the entrepreneur's options at an instant in time. Yet since technological progress can be thought of as economizing on one or more factors of production, it can be indirectly depicted by a second curve B B' closer to the origin of the two axes.

Now if we were to treat information as a factor of production in its own right, it would not do to simply add it to existing factors of production and then to treat it as just another dimension in the diagram. Why? Because information is already latently present in productive factors such as capital and labour in the form of know-how and experience: in the case of capital such information is expressed in the design and performance of machinery and equipment; in the case of labour it shows up as technical skills and adapted behaviour patterns. By keeping the other factors unchanged, therefore, we would in most cases be double counting.

In claiming that it is information that is latently present in capital and labour we are in fact guilty of loose talk. Information is not a thing but a pattern that is perceived in a set of data, a pattern that has to be extracted from the data by a data processing agent. What is latent in a traditional factor of production, then, is not information *per se* but *data*, and it is therefore data that has to be treated as a factor of production.

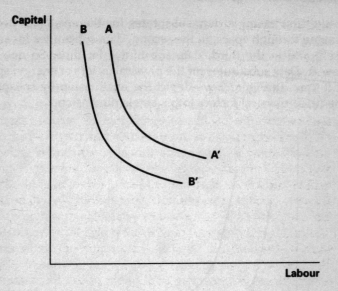

Figure 1 *A Traditional Production Function.*

So how should other factors of production be modified to allow data into the picture?

A New Production Function

Another way of posing the question is to ask what data substitutes for in productive activity? In no particular order, here are three pointers to a reply:

- In the aftermath of the most recent earthquake in San Francisco, many people who could not drive their cars to work sat in front of their PCs and telecommuted.

- Nissan has experimentally manufactured an internal combustion engine smaller than a pinhead.

- The fastest 486 microprocessor operates at 54 million instructions per second (mips); Digital's new Alpha microprocessor is claimed to have a speed of 200 mips.

In the first example data substitutes for the energy of bodies moving through space; in the second, data substitutes for space itself; and in the third, data substitutes for time. So now we have it. Data substitutes for the physical factors of energy, space and time. In Figure 2 we depict the relationship by collapsing the three physical factors into a single dimension.

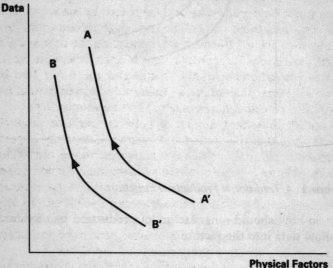

Figure 2 *A New Production Function.*

Although Figure 2 looks identical to Figure 1, appearances are deceptive. Consider, by way of example, movement along the horizontal and vertical axes in each diagram. In the case of capital and labour (Figure 1), moving either up or to the right is straightforward; it involves increasing the consumption of each factor in a linear fashion. The costs of such consumption then go up proportionately, providing that the factors are competitively priced. In the case of the physical factors depicted in Figure 2, a rightward move is likewise straightforward. So is moving back towards the origin: one simply consumes less of the physical factors.

Are movements along the data axis equally simple? How are

we to interpret, for example, a doubling of data inputs into the productive process? Do we expect the price of this data to vary proportionately with increased consumption? And what does it mean to *reduce* the data inputs into the production process?

We need not try to answer these questions here. The key point to be made is that data is not subject to the same kind of *scarcities* as physical factors are. In the world of physical objects you cannot have your cake and eat it too. In the world of data you can – and there will still be enough (for good or ill) for the neighbours. Baking the cake, i.e. generating the data in the first place, may be costly; reproducing it is often little more than the cost of photocopying. If the loaves and the fishes had been electronic rather than physical, their multiplication would today have been considered a somewhat less impressive feat.

Another important difference between the two production functions is that the second one offers a potentially important insight into cultural evolution. It allows cultural evolution to be represented as a process of substituting data for the physical resources of energy, space and time across the whole spectrum of human activity. Data accumulates in physical and biological systems *through learning and memorization* and this leads to a gradual reduction in physical resources consumed and hence to a movement over time along curve A A′ of Figure 2.

There is of course a limit to how much data – complexity by any other name – a physical or biological system can deal with before it gets overwhelmed. Close to that limit, such a system will be concerned with saving on data as well as on physical resources, and saving on data of course means moving down the vertical axis of Figure 2 and on to curve B B′. As with Figure 1, this shift of curve involves a discontinuity: *saving on data means essentially extracting information from it, in the form of patterns and insights; it means in effect generating new knowledge.* The creation of new knowledge, therefore, is nothing but a strategy for reducing complexity.

Figure 3 offers a highly schematic representation of the evolutionary production function at work. It depicts three major knowledge revolutions that have shaped the development of our species: firstly, the neolithic revolution which occurred ten thousand years ago and marked the transition from hunting and gathering to a settled agriculture[4] through a systematic exploitation of renewable energy resources; secondly, the industrial revolution which marked the transition from an agricultural to an industrial economy based on a scientific mastery of non-renewable energy resources; finally, the information revolution which we are still living through and which involves a shift from an energy-based to a knowledge-based economy.

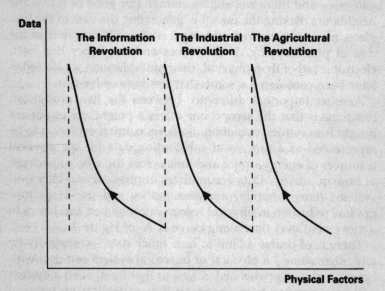

Figure 3 *Evolutionary Production Function.*

Our new production function throws into sharp relief the point made by Peter Drucker which amounts to this: we have an economics for the horizontal axis of Figure 3 but not yet for the vertical axis; we understand the production and exchange of things that we can drop on our feet and that occupy a distinct location in space and in time, but not the production and exchange of things as elusive as knowledge.

The basic message of this book is that the production and exchange of knowledge are above all *cultural* activities, and that in order to come to grips with them the tools of anthropology will be at least as important as those of economics. In the next five chapters we develop an anthropologically oriented analytical framework through which to explore the production and exchange of information within and between groups. And since this book is aimed at the practising manager as much as at the theoretician, the use of the framework will then be illustrated by applying it to enterprise problems at various levels.

The Structure of the Book

We shall proceed as follows: the structuring of information, the process of perceptual and conceptual articulation through which an individual gradually learns to make sense of his world, will be the focus of the next chapter; the way this information is socially shared and diffused among different social groupings will then form the subject of Chapter Two. The first two chapters do little more than set the stage for our analysis by providing first, the psychological and second, the sociological foundations for a simple yet fundamental communication relationship that is presented in Chapter Three. In a sense, this chapter is the heart of the matter, the conceptual core around which the rest of the book is built up. By showing that a systematic relationship exists between the way information is structured and the way it is shared, we open the door to a much more extensive application of cultural anthropology than has been possible until now. Chapter Four sets the insights developed in Chapter Three and places them in a dynamic context. Information structuring and sharing is examined as a process evolving in time. Up until this point, the discussion is essentially abstract. Examples, to be sure, drawn from the real world are provided and, since this book is addressed to the practising manager, they are drawn as far as possible from the world of management. But we are not yet in the world of managerial anthropology. The *rites de passage* occur in Chapter Five when a number of the key social relationships associated with different communication strategies are identified and explored. Although we shall argue that these are pretty well universal, their relevance to managerial concerns will become quickly apparent.

Part One of the book, then, is essentially theory.

Part Two explores specific areas of application of the theory presented in Part One. In Chapter Six, we take the concepts presented in the abstract and embed them in the firm. We are still in the world of theory but of focused theory. Chapter Seven uses the theory to explore the firm's deployment of its technological assets. Chapter Eight building on its predecessor, explores some organizational problems of the firm in the light of our newly-created concepts and, as a natural extension of this, the scope of the firm is scrutinized in Chapter Nine: when should the firm make things for itself and when should it collaborate with others? What form should this collaboration take and what might be expected from it? In Chapter Ten, the international operations of the enterprise are examined through our anthropological lens, and here we shall find that areas, which until now were considered rather fuzzy, suddenly come into focus.

The next two chapters of the book bring together the different strands of our analysis to give a very specific meaning to the term 'corporate culture'. In Chapter Eleven, we submit to the imperative of fashion and take another look at the Japanese firm. Like others, we ask whether Japanese managerial practices are moving closer to western ones or are destined to remain forbiddingly opaque and alien. Chapter Twelve places the issue of corporate culture in a new and unexpected context – that of a rapidly evolving national culture. In that chapter, we shall look at the problems of enterprise reform in the People's Republic of China. If managerial anthropology is to claim a wider generality than the more culture-specific disciplines of organization behaviour or industrial sociology, then surely modernizing China is *par excellence* the laboratory in which its crucial experiments must be devised.

The concluding chapter, Thirteen, is an invitation to reflect on what managerial anthropology has to offer the practising manager in the information age. In fact, the chapter takes us beyond management to ask a number of leading questions about the nature of information in general. The reader is invited to peer over the horizon, and into the neighbouring territory of political economy.

To summarize, this book presents a new body of concepts, or less modestly, a theory, if you will, and explores their implication in, and sometimes beyond, the field of management. If we have chosen to call the outcome managerial anthropology, it is because the concepts, at least in their formative stages, bear more than a passing resemblance to those used by anthropologists to describe culture.[5] Some anthropologists may shudder at seeing their conceptual progenies straying into the executive boardrooms from the Amazonian rain forests where they have been reared. But would they not be the first to agree that travel broadens the mind?

References
1. Braudel, F., *Civilisation Matérielle, Economie et Capitalisme au XVe–XVIIIe Siècle; Les Structures du Quotidien*, Paris: Armand Colin, 1979.
2. Kroeber, A. and Kluckhohn, C., *Culture: A Critical Review of Concepts and Definitions*. Papers of the Peabody Museums of American Archaeology and Ethnology, Vol. 47, Cambridge: Harvard University Press, 1952.
3. Drucker, P., *Post-Capitalist Society*, Oxford: Butterworth-Heinemann, 1993.
4. North, D., *Structure and Change in Economic History*, New York: W. W. Norton and Co., 1981.
5. See, for example, Douglas, M., *Natural Symbols: Explorations in Cosmology*, Middlesex: Penguin Books, 1973.

PART ONE

Concepts

1

The Structuring of Information

Introduction

Proposition 7 of Wittgenstein's *Tractatus Logico-Philosophicus*, the last one in his Book, holds that 'what we cannot speak about, we must pass over in silence'.[1] Everyday experience refutes this assertion. Wittgenstein had not had the opportunity of meeting Mrs Lucach, my ex-landlady, or my five-year-old daughter, both past masters of the saucy wink and the suggestive nudge. In fact, it is clear to me that their non-verbal gestures connote, or are meant to connote, different things. My ex-landlady is on the permanent lookout for fellow conspirators sufficiently 'in the know' to detect, in her ribald signallings, intimations of dark malpractices which they are invited to partake of. My daughter's own expressive efforts are not (yet) of this kind, being little more than a primitive form of plea-bargaining usually entered into under compromising circumstances – a face stuffed with chocolate or sweets falling out from under her sweater. As a general rule, I have little trouble decoding the messages each of them is sending to me.

Communication as Coding

For, of course, that is exactly what each is doing: communicating in a code and implicitly assuming that the context in which we interact is sufficiently clear to both of us to make up for any deficiencies in the sign system itself. My daughter's wink is not my landlady's wink and only a fool or a maniac would take it for such. The physical act of winking is inherently ambiguous and requires a context to perform effectively as a sign. Perhaps, in the case of my daughter, if we did not share this context –

our kinship, the house we both live in, her knowledge of what I feel about her eating chocolate and sweets – she may hesitate to wink. Perhaps, then she might not deliberately communicate at all. Indeed, if she failed to, she may blush, thus involuntarily conveying an inability to summon up an adequate communicative response to justify her situation. But in neither case is she likely to try to verbalize what her wink was intended to convey: 'Hello, daddy, you have just caught me doing something that I shouldn't be doing when I least expected it, and since I have no way of escaping any punishment that you have it in your power to mete out to me, my only hope is to charm you into leniency by being frail and feminine and making you feel rotten if you behave too harshly towards me, the daughter you love and cherish'. It simply would not wash. She might get away with a wink and a nudge, just. She would not get away with its verbal equivalent.

Thus effective communication requires that we choose the right code. In an auction room, a wink shrewdly conveyed will secure a Cézanne; in a court of law, aimed at the judge, it will add six months to a prison sentence. Since only a few of these codes involve speech or writing, we remain for the most part unaware of the extent to which our daily life is shot through with codes. One does not ski in a dinner jacket or shave in the subway. Tap dancing at board meetings compromises one's promotion prospects and distributing peppermints to the workforce smacks of a frivolous paternalism. To complicate matters, when we do use codes we use them in combination – we shake hands *and* we smile as we say 'How do you do?' Remove one of those three elements and the experience of a greeting changes its spots. A shift of meaning occurs.

Choosing the Code

Sometimes, of course, our choice of codes is restricted by the circumstances in which we interact. I cannot pour you a whisky over the telephone to make you feel at home, and a letter to my loved one is no substitute for a tête à tête at Maxim's. When I phone someone or if I write to them, I use different conventions from those I would use when gestures and proximity are available to eliminate ambiguity and misunderstanding. Even within the written medium, the common prior experiences I share with friends and relatives allow an altogether less formal, more implicit, communication style than that I will allow myself when writing to the faceless bureaucrats of the French PTTs in order to question the details of my phone bill. After all, to them I have no face either, and must make up for this deficiency in my choice of phrases.

Perhaps the most ambitious attempt to reduce the full range of human experience to a single code remains James Joyce's *Ulysses* – twenty-four hours in the life of one man packed into eight hundred odd pages. They are not equivalent offerings nor were they intended to be. Art is never simply an imitation of nature but also a commentary upon it. Would anyone, asked casually what he did yesterday, pour forth eight hundred pages' worth of narrative? *Ulysses* is not a natural form of communication. If anything, it is a limiting case of communication, in which the author's intentions appear submerged in his own stream of consciousness.

So how, then, does one choose the form in which to communicate? The question, I believe, has two answers which must be clearly distinguished. The first is that we can only chose from a repertoire of codes that is already available to us – i.e. we must first master the codes we wish to use. I cannot tell you how pleased I am to meet you if I do not speak your language. I can only smile and hope that my facial expression reads the same way for you as it does for me. As anyone who has travelled to the Far East will know this cannot always be assumed. The second is that we have a natural tendency to use that code which requires the least effort from us for a given effect. Assuming that the repertoire is available to us and to others, we prefer the wink to the long verbal explanation unless the context is such that the wink could be misunderstood. But even here, we shall probably use a combination of codes – the wink with, say, a few words rather than rely on the more ponderous effect of words alone. The choice of code is in large part an intuitive one and it is only in those situations where problems are anticipated that acts of communication are subjected to any process of rational deliberation.

Coding and Memory

It is often overlooked that codes have a dual function. They help us to give structure to our experience *and* they enable us to communicate it. Experiences which cannot be structured to some degree cannot be communicated, they can only be *shared*. No written description by me of a later Rembrandt self portrait will ever replace your direct contemplation of the work. Once you have seen it, of course, then we could talk about it; we have a shared experience that helps to calibrate our messages.

But the structured experience itself has to achieve a certain stability if it is to crystallize into communicable signs and symbols. The fleeting sensation is hard to capture and even harder to describe, passing through us like a light breeze below the threshold of awareness. Encoding an experience not only gives it structure, but casts it in a form that can be stored in memory and hence stabilized, making it accessible for subsequent retrieval even if the form in which it is recalled and maybe expressed is not that in which it was initially apprehended. The way you live through significant events as a child and the way you recall them are two different things. And what you can then say about them is something else again. Thus there is nothing passive about memory as a store of past experiences. What is currently encoded in the store acts upon what comes into the store and is in turn modified by it. What I see when I now visit London, what attracts my notice and comments, is in large part the product of what I remember London to be. Prior expectation crowds out innocent observation. The past is forever colliding with the present and imprinting itself upon it. We are only fully conscious of the process when it is external to us, but it occurs within us as well.

Private Versus Public Knowledge

The codes we use to *structure* experience can be private ones. If I choose to encode the billowing cloud of coloured dots impinging on my retina as an elephant and you make it out to be a tree, then as long as I keep my thought to myself, there is little that you can do about it. But as soon as I use my coding repertoire to *communicate* my experience, then I must needs make certain assumptions about what you see as well. Unless we both see trees or elephants, then we do not speak the same language. We may devise rules that transpose elephants into trees and vice versa so that some limited communication can take place between us but I will go on seeing elephants and you will go on seeing trees. Our respective experiences will remain for the most part incommunicable – what Michael Polanyi has called *personal knowledge.*[2] A perceptual event exists out there whose existence we both acknowledge but which we each register in different ways through coding practices that are personal to us.

Public knowledge, by contrast, can only be built up through a stock of shared codes. A public event, then, is one which a group of people agree to code for in the same way: a football match, a scientific discovery, the Houses of Parliament, and so on. But this does not mean that personal knowledge is altogether absent. The way that you know a football match will depend on whether you are a player or a spectator. A scientific discovery does not have the same meaning for the casual reader of its announcement in a scientific journal and for the one who does the discovering after twenty years of arduous searching. The Houses of Parliament yield less to the gaze of a tourist from Nebraska than to those who work there. Yet in all these examples more can be communicated concerning the event than is the case with strictly private knowledge, and it will for the most part be readily understood and unproblematic.

The shared codes of public knowledge are those which have been built up over time and have withstood extensive interpersonal testing. Personal knowledge may be no less valid – all public knowledge initially starts out as the idiosyncratic insight of an individual – but it is altogether more transient, biographically articulated, and hence fragile and perishable. Fewer systematically developed codes are available to capture the rich and varied stream of personal or private events. Just what exactly is it, for example, about a familiar face that allows you to recognize it in less time than it takes to snap your fingers? Try now to describe that face to someone who has never seen it before in sufficient detail to enable him to pick it out in a crowd. How long will it take you? How confident are you of success? If you were skilled with a pencil, you might try sketching the face or, better still, you might provide a photograph. After all, a picture is worth a thousand words. Why?

Because a photograph operates at a lower level of coding than a verbal description, as a message it is richer in information and therefore offers more to chew on. A cartoon sketch is halfway between the two, picking out an individual's salient features and depicting them in a few summary lines. A cartoon gains much of its impact from the fact that the original is known and can be recognized through the lines that represent him, but to pick out the original from the cartoon alone would be quite a different matter. Hence the degree to which a message *can* be coded turns not only on the prior sharing of codes as we have already seen, but also on the prior availability of shared experience between sender and receiver. Much humour, for example, to be effective requires a shared context between a comedian and his audience. Punchlines operate on a set of implicit premises that only require a single gesture or a word to trigger off laughter. Much humour, however, does not travel well across national boundaries. Implicit premises are locked up within a specific language or a cultural tradition. Will Rogers' quip that 'a man who hates kids can't be all bad' is not always thought to be a universal truth, and will be tiresomely scrutinized and debated in some cultures.

Coding as Selection

But what is meant exactly by a *lower* coding level? And why is a lower coding level associated with a richer level of information? An example will help to address these questions. If I were the personnel manager of a company and I wanted to talk to a divisional manager about a prospective employee, I could refer to him in several ways, depending on circumstances. I could, for instance, ask him to be physically present and literally designate him with my finger. Here I am not coding at all and merely inviting the divisional manager to share my direct experience of the candidate's physical presence but, in this case, although the information available on the candidate is then at its richest, it is co-extensive with his presence. Should he be unavailable, information about him will have to be gleaned more selectively – and *to select is to code*. Perhaps I will have the candidate on videotape, offering an experience still rich in information but now pre-programmed and less flexible and hence informative than a face-to-face interview might be. Now if the divisional director is pressed for time (perhaps there are several candidates to process at this stage) he may pursue his deliberations on the basis of an application form and the candidate's résumé alone. The information available to him then becomes more selective still and he now has to balance the value of the time saved against that of the information lost at this higher – i.e. more selective – level of coding. A résumé compresses a vast amount of biographical information into a few well-chosen symbols on one or two sheets of paper. Anyone with any experience of the recruiting process will be aware of the gap that frequently exists between what can be communicated in coded form by a candidate 'on paper' and what comes across 'live' in an unstructured interview. And those familiar with the hazards of computer dating will have their own stories to tell.

Finally, and to complete our example, we might imagine that we are in the early stages of a recruiting campaign and that we are only required to make a pre-selection of candidates for later consideration. In that case, we can be even more selective and simply classify candidates by age, region, and qualifications, and apply the coding scheme presented in the first column of Table 1.1 in a sequential manner to the remaining three columns. Thus, to illustrate, 3–3–5 would describe a candidate in his twenties, of Asian origin, and with a high school diploma. We are operating on a higher, more selective, level of coding than the résumé, with a greater loss of information richness but with compensating gains in the speed at which information can be subsequently processed.

Table 1.1 *Coding Sheet for Candidate Classification*

Code No	Age	Region	Educational Qualification
1	–10	America	Doctorate Degree
2	11–20	Europe	Master's Degree
3	21–30	Asia	Bachelor's Degree
4	31–40	Middle East	Junior College Diploma
5	41–50	Africa	High School Diploma
6	51–60	Australasia	Primary School Diploma

Example: Candidate 3–3–5: Age 21–30, Asian, High School Diploma.

To summarize: at the lowest coding level, the direct experience of the candidate himself is the message and no compression of information takes place. At the highest coding level, the candidate is compressed into a few symbols and the resulting loss of information makes him unrecognizable – even to his friends. Which level of coding you wish to apprehend the candidate on depends on your intentions. To justify the recruitment of the chief executive of General Motors on the grounds that he is a 5–1–1 in the table may not cut much ice with flesh and blood shareholders whose life savings are invested in the company. Recruiting at this level is a time-consuming operation that can run into months, if not years, and that requires extensive face-to-face interaction.

A Coding Scale

Different coding levels can be represented as points on a scale, running from 0 to 1, that describe how far a given message can be compressed into symbols (see Figure 1.1). The scale is constructed using the reciprocal of the number of bits (binary digits) needed to transmit a message of a given length. The zero point at the bottom of the scale, then, represents one over infinity ($^1/\infty$), that mystical condition in which *no* number of symbols can ever exhaust the message. We have in $^1/\infty = 0$ an ineffable experience which cannot be structured and is condemned to resonate in 'silence' within a single mind. It might, in exceptional circumstances, be *shared* and thus become an occasion for fellowship among a small band of initiates, but it can never be *communicated*. Zen practices, the spiritual exercise of St Ignatius of Loyola, and the sacred mushroom peyote, each offers a different avenue to such shared experiences.

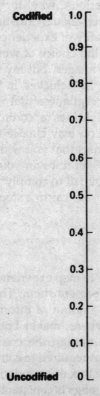

Figure 1.1 *A Coding Scale $\frac{1}{N \text{ BITS}}$.*

At the top of the scale, the message, whatever its length, can be compressed into a single symbol, say, a 0 or a 1, so that $^1/_1 = 1$. No further compression of that particular message is possible without expanding its content, combining it with other messages, and so on.

Most everyday communication activities, of course, involve points on the coding scale between these two extremes. We are not struck dumb by most experiences that we encounter, nor do we master them to the point of reducing them to a single solitary sign. If the latter were the case we might, paradoxically, find ourselves once more in the mystical realm. There is something ineffable about the cross as a religious symbol to worshippers because in a mysterious way it does compress everything they know and feel about Christianity. But this power to *connote*, to map a plurality of experiences onto a single sign, lacks any precision. A skilful choice of words by the poet can evoke varied and powerful images, but my images will not be your images, so that what he achieves in scope he loses in control. Contrast the poetic vagueness that results with the semantic precision of traffic lights as a coding system. Red means stop, green means go. You may choose to associate the red of a traffic light with the sunset that you witnessed last year in the Grand Canyon, but this will not win you any friends in a court of law if, in doing so, you fail to comply with its socially established meaning and bring your car to a stop as required by the highway code.

Coding as Mapping

A coding skill, then, is an ability to map experiences on to appropriate sign systems that will represent them. This compression into symbols, by reducing the amount of information one has to carry in one's head or elsewhere, makes both thinking and communication possible, even though the coding required to structure one's thoughts and that required to communicate them are not always the same. In the flux of an individual's personal experience, for example, many objects can stand for each other as signs. The barn door stands for the quarrel that I had with my younger sister when I was eight years old, and my two and a half years at MIT are condensed into a vision of the domes above the Institution's main entrance on 'Mass Av.'. But talking of barn doors and MIT's domes will not evoke the same memory in my neighbour. They are private codes, a shorthand for the recollection and further processing of intensely personal experiences that are for the most part incommunicable in their richness, save perhaps to those who have shared in them. Public codes are altogether more constraining both as to what they refer to and as to how. They are designed to facilitate the communication rather than the structuring of experience and are built up gradually through a process of consensus and by common usage. As we shall see later, in the hands of creative individuals, private codes may sometimes evolve into public ones. We shall defer discussion of this complex process to Chapter Four.

Coding as a Classification of Experience

Every living moment, we are bombarded with stimuli from the outside world, the vast majority of which we are more or less forced to ignore. Those we attend to are assigned to different categories that express for the most part snap judgements concerning our environment. Thus, for example, at this moment I can hear a number of hissing, whining and rattling sounds which through long experience I resolve into the noise made by my refrigerator. The process is automatic, mostly unconscious, and pretty well describes the way we each habitually code our world. Yet the habitual way of coding may not always be the appropriate way. For some purposes, the coding effort may have to be more deliberate and reflective. Suppose for a moment that I were an assembly line quality control inspector in a refrigerator manufacturing plant. I might then choose to code for refrigerators in a number of different ways and at different levels. I might for example code for the presence or absence of certain components by ticking them off on a checklist on a chart. More intuitively, I could 'eyeball' the quality of the paintwork relying on prior experience to tell me when a given sample is 'off-colour'. Finally, I could test the product's thermal performance by taking temperature readings at various points and in different circumstances.

In this way, I might systematically summarize my experience of the refrigerator through a purposeful combination of high and low level codes as in Figure 1.2, building up a complex description of the object much of which may only be considered meaningful in a manufacturing context and therefore only communicable within that context. As a consumer, my coding resources are likely to be much more limited and to operate at a lower, more verbose, level. The fridge 'makes a funny sound' and maybe 'is not as cold as it should be' – witness the watery ice box. If I call in the repairman my lack of coding capacity is quickly brought home to me by the ease with which the correct technical term rolls off his tongue. Doctors, as an occupational category, I have noticed, do not always resist the temptation to reduce their patients to a state of abject dependency by skilful application of their power to classify them. What is diagnosis after all if not the coding of symptoms into useful categories? To code or classify is always in some sense to assert control. The first real power given to a child over his world is that of naming things. Before that, the only power he has – and a modest one it is as any nappy-harassed mother will argue – is over his own movements and bodily states.

Mastering the Coding Process

To sum up the discussion so far, the coding resources available to us along the scale will strongly influence our manner of apprehending our world. To be without speech is not simply to be deprived of ways of talking about the world with our neighbours. It is to construct a world that will radically differ from theirs. But, if this is true for speech, it also holds for smell, and for numbers. An individual rich in coding resources is one capable of operating effectively from different points on the coding scale, and of moving when appropriate from one point to another. Take, for example, an art critic, someone who, receiving from a work of art stimuli at a comparatively low level

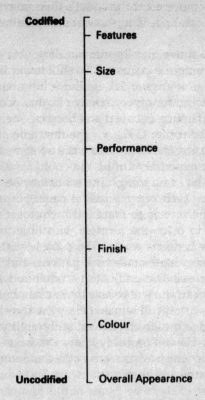

Figure 1.2 *Coding a Refrigerator on the Scale.*

of coding, can convert them into stimuli at a higher level of coding. He selectively transforms purely visual signs into written ones. In so doing, he performs an act of interpretation for those unfamiliar with the lower level code, thus rendering it intelligible. But, as was suggested earlier, in doing so he also sacrifices information. He selects, and all selection implies rejection. Some of his own personal experience of the work of art will be lost in the translation. It may not amount to much, but only he can be the judge of that, never his lay audience.

The art critic, in restructuring and communicating his experience to others, moves up the coding scale towards higher level codes. Is it possible to move *down* the coding scale from higher level to lower level codes and, if so, how should this be interpreted?

At first sight, such a move may appear puzzling. Are we not being invited to de-structure experience? To shift towards a less communicable mode? The answer is yes, and a little reflection will show that there is nothing very strange in this. Consider for a moment the difference between a schoolboy seeing the chemical formula for benzene, C_6H_6, for the first time and the professional chemist using the formula to write up some laboratory notes on a recent experiment of his. In contemplating the symbols do they see the same thing? The schoolboy sees a set of symbols that follow each other across a page. He may be somewhat aware of the principles that bind them together but he will initially have to learn the formula with little intuitive understanding of how benzene works. The professional chemist, by contrast, will see the formula as a pattern, and have a sixth sense as to its possibilities. Like the schoolboy who has learnt the formula by heart, he will be able to repeat it, but much of what he associates with it will remain below the threshold of awareness as knowledge intuitively arrived at through years of dealing with benzene. He will probably know almost unconsciously, for instance, in which of the aromatic compounds the benzene grouping of atoms is likely to show up and what their chemical properties are likely to be. Some of this knowledge he will be able to put down on paper and so communicate it to others but at a level of compression that falls well short of that achieved by the formula itself. Much of what he knows about benzene, however, is destined to remain personal to him, uncodifiable and hence incommunicable.

A move down the coding scale increases the ambiguity of experience and makes it less certain. The less it is coded, the greater the scope for varied and subjective interpretations that may express impulses and motivations projected into the experience rather than derived from it. One who persists in seeing elephants rather than foliage when contemplating trees is likely to be projecting an unconscious fear of elephants in all his perceptions; and, if others detect a rich heiress behind every

The Structuring of Information

feminine smile, it may be symptomatic of little more than the problems they habitually face in meeting their quarterly telephone bill when it falls due.

Personality factors powerfully affect the way we seek to articulate our experiences. Some people, confronted with fuzzy, ambiguous stimuli, experience anxiety and a need for closure. They feel happier operating further up the coding scale where spades are spades and not grasshoppers or crème caramel. Engineers and accountants often feel more comfortable working with well-defined problems in which a limited number of variables can be manipulated to yield known and reliable solutions – the optimal span for a bridge, the least risky ratio of debt to equity for a firm – than they do navigating through eddies and whirlpools of issues in which real problems cannot be distinguished from will-o'-the-wisp ones and where both are rapidly submerged in a torrential flow of variables as soon as they appear. Artists, architects and entrepreneurs, on the other hand, may positively thrive in such cognitive habitats, and judge balance sheets to be a dull and tiresome business compared with the thrill of following up the half-formulated hunch or the suggestive lead. Most people fall somewhere between these two extremes, enjoying uncertainty and ambiguity in some situations and preferring structure in others.

Recent brain research points to a biological basis for these coding preferences. Although I do not wish to put this forward here as any more than a suggestion, much of the recent work that associates the right side of the brain with artistic ability and the left side with rationality and verbalization could be reformulated as propositions concerning their different coding propensities. They would then appear as in Figure 1.3 with possibly some overlap between them.

Are such coding preferences learnt or are they innate and immutable? If the answer is that they are learnt, then one would expect processes of socialization and acculturation to favour particular points on the scale. Although work on the right and left side of the brain has highlighted the influence of language and culture in brain development, we shall defer discussion of this question to Chapters Eleven and Twelve where the reciprocal

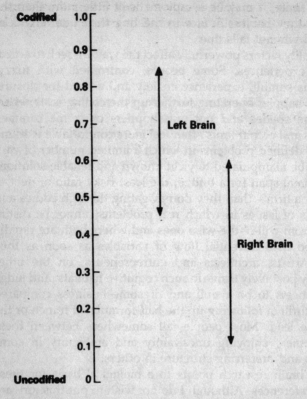

Figure 1.3 *Coding Propensities of the Left and Right Brain.*

influence that culture and cognition exert on each other will be more closely examined.

Conclusion

In this chapter, neither management nor anthropology have been much in evidence. We are still in the foothills of our analysis and will have to climb further before our gaze commands any worthwhile territory. Yet our discussion of information structuring has moved us forward. The next chapter, on information sharing, is the natural complement to this one. By

Chapter Three, we shall already be well into anthropological issues and by Chapter Four we shall be training our sights on managerial issues.

References

1. Wittgenstein, L., *Tractatus Logico-Philosophicus*, London: Routledge and Kegan Paul, 1961.
2. Polanyi, M., *Personal Knowledge: Towards a Post-Critical Philosophy*, London: Routledge and Kegan Paul, 1958.

Information Sharing

Introduction

In the preceding chapter, we looked at how the coding of information helped to structure experience and how it rendered it more communicable. The emphasis was essentially on the communicating *individual* receiving and responding to a variety of stimuli. In this chapter, we shall focus on the communication *relationship* rather than on the isolated individual, on the sociological aspects of information sharing rather than on the psychological ones of information structuring. Coding, of course, is common to both and therefore acts as an important link between what goes on inside one mind and cannot be directly observed, and what goes on between minds, which can.

We shall begin by discussing the communication process at the most general level and identifying a number of key requirements for effective communications. In doing this, we shall follow a well trodden path. But as we progress some less obvious features of the communication relationship will emerge to enrich our discussion in Chapter Three.

A Communication Model

A good point of departure might be the simple communication model shown in Figure 2.1. It presents us with a limited number of elements which most readers will be familiar with.

1 *A source*: the mind or minds in which a message originates.

2 *A transmitter*: the physical device used for transmitting the message. As I write these lines, the transmitter is my hand

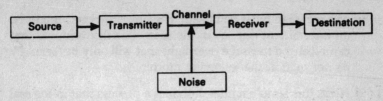

Figure 2.1 *A Simple Communication Model.*

holding the pen. If I were to speak, it would be my voice. A message cannot simply be pushed through a transmitter as it stands. It must be put into a form that the transmitter can handle. I therefore *encode* my message through the use of graphic symbols as I write, or through phonetic utterances if I am talking.

3 *A channel*: the message must travel through some medium – sight, sound, touch, and so on – if it is to reach its destination. What I write can remain as such on the paper and can then be physically dispatched from one corner of the globe to the other or, alternatively, it could be typed up and sent by telex over the airwaves. This would involve a new transmitter, a new code, and a new channel. If I speak, my voice can travel directly to a destination no more than a few feet away through sound waves or it can be converted into electrical signals and transmitted over greater distances by means of radio waves.

4 *A receiver*: the soundwaves produced by my voice bounce aimlessly off the stone floor and expend themselves uselessly on the grass outside my open window. They only contribute to an act of communication if they are picked up by a receiver that can reproduce the message as originally encoded. Your eyes and ears are receivers, so are my television set and my telephone.

5 *A destination*: the mind or minds that a message is aimed at. Again, as with transmission, the message is picked up by the receiver, and must be *decoded* to be intelligible to a destination. Clearly the receiver and the final destination

of a message must be linked. The link, however, might be an intermittent one, as in the case of a telex terminal that can receive a message overnight that will only be 'seen' by its destination the following morning.

6 *Noise*: this simple model describes a process that in the real world works with varying degrees of efficiency. The signals that crowd in upon us at any moment are not orderly and often mask each other, acting as a source of *noise* to messages that we want someone to hear or that someone wants us to hear. If, for example, I am whispering sweet nothings into the ear of my loved one as the 8.15 from Manchester roars past my window, I may have to repeat what I said with some considerable loss of effect. *Redundancy* in communication then becomes a necessary compensation for the information lost through noise. Too much redundancy, however, and the message sinks from attention under the weight of its own dullness. The classic example is the case of the child crying 'wolf' so often that when the genuine article turns up nobody notices.

Shannon's Three Communication Problems

The trick in communicating effectively, therefore, is one of striking a balance between offering so little redundancy that a message becomes unintelligible and so much that it becomes banal. Yet much will depend on the skill of the destination and its prior expectations rather than on the message source. Claude Shannon and Warren Weaver,[1] in their classic paper on the mathematical theory of communication, identify three types of problem that must be overcome if effective communication is to take place at all.

1 The Technical Problem
Is the message received the same as the message sent? If not, then there is noise in the channel and information loss. Imagine a rain-soaked letter with a pale blue blot masquer-

ading as an address. One or two letters can still be picked out but the rest is indecipherable. What is a postman to do? By building in some redundancy into the message – for instance by repeating the destination address both on the back of the envelope and on the writing paper inside the envelope – one can reduce the chance of faulty transmission. By writing the sender's address on the envelope as well, one also creates an opportunity to re-transmit if the need arises.

2 The Semantic Problem

Is the message received understood? Does the destination possess the coding skills necessary to decode it? The letter may reach its destination all right but if the sender wrote in Arabic and the reader does not speak Arabic, then either he has to find someone to translate it for him (which is tedious) or he has to go out and register for evening courses in Arabic (which is even more tedious). Of course, he could always toss the letter away, in which case no communication has taken place.

3 The Effectiveness Problem

Does the message lead to the desired behaviour? I receive a letter, I understand every word, but it turns out to be one of those personalized mailshots inviting me to a week's free trial of Kennomeat for my fox terrier. If I neither possess a fox terrier nor have close relatives partial to Kennomeat, the letter will still end up in the waste paper basket, a wasted effort. The effectiveness of a mailshot usually depends on how much information the advertiser can glean about me and my habits beforehand. These will give him clues concerning my prior expectations and probable response.

Effectiveness requires some knowledge of the destination.

A few points are in order concerning Shannon and Weaver's three problems. First, you rarely confront problems of communication effectiveness unless you have successfully overcome the technical and semantic problems. Likewise, you do not usually hit the semantic problem unless you have cleared the technical level problems. The question of whether or not I decide to buy Kennomeat for my terrier will not arise if I never receive the letter, or – in my case at least – if it is written in Russian.

Second, approaches to the three types of problem vary considerably: the technical problem can only be dealt with by looking at the physical characteristics of the communication elements that make up the system; the semantic problem, on the other hand, can only be overcome by having the communicating parties investing in common set of codes; finally, the effectiveness problem is, in the main, one of sensing expectations, attitudes and beliefs of the communicating parties.

Third, noise operates at all three levels and not just at the technical level. As was pointed out in Chapter One, what I already know may interfere with what you are trying to tell me to distort the way I receive your message. Semantic noise is pervasive in human relationships and leads to the well known 'Here she goes again' syndrome in marriages heading for a communication breakdown. Also, and more intractable, prior personal beliefs and preferences can filter messages with strange results, so that civil rights workers are branded as 'soft on communism', and multinational corporations 'lackeys of US Imperialism'. Not all communications specialists would subscribe to this stretched application of the term 'noise', but it seems as good a word as any to describe the distorting influence that prior knowledge and values held by a destination can exert on the communication process as a whole.

Finally, it should be clear from what has been said that effective communication does not consist of reproducing in the mind of a destination a carbon copy of what is in the mind of a message source. What flows between the two is information, and the way that it embeds itself in the mind of one destination may well differ radically from the way the same information affects his neighbour. The effectiveness of a communication act can only be inferred from the behaviour of the parties, and two message recipients might behave in identical fashion after hearing someone shout 'Fire!' and yet still experience the message in radically different ways. Effective communication is above all meaningful communication and a message only has meaning for someone if it modifies to some degree, no matter how small, his expectations and preference concerning the world, and his disposition to act in it. That said, a message can be meaningful without being effective if it has some effect on the receiver that undermines that intended by the sender. Much political propaganda and many poorly thought out advertising campaigns are of this nature.

Communication Networks

As presented here, our communication model deals with one source and one destination, the most elementary communicative relationship imaginable. We can easily extend the model to deal with one source and several destinations, several sources and one destination, several sources and several destinations (Figure 2.2). More complicated is the situation in which a destination is also a source and acts as a relay (Figure 2.3). Through such successive overlays we move from simple to highly complex communication processes, in which new problems appear that are not addressed at the level of the simple model.

An extensive literature exists on the relative efficiency of different communication patterns involving small and large groups.[2] Space does not allow us to discuss it here nor is it immediately relevant to our purpose. We shall instead develop a simple communication diffusion scale around which we can build our analysis of information sharing behaviour. Figure 2.4 describes a cumulative scale along which a given population can be distributed, with zero per cent of the population receiving the message on the extreme left hand point of the scale and one hundred per cent receiving it on the extreme right hand point. Population size at this stage is not specified. It could consist of twelve people or of twelve million. With equal intervals along the scale, the technical conditions of communication are assumed to be uniform throughout the population. People are all equally distributed through space and can communicate with equal facility – if one has a telephone, all of them have it, and

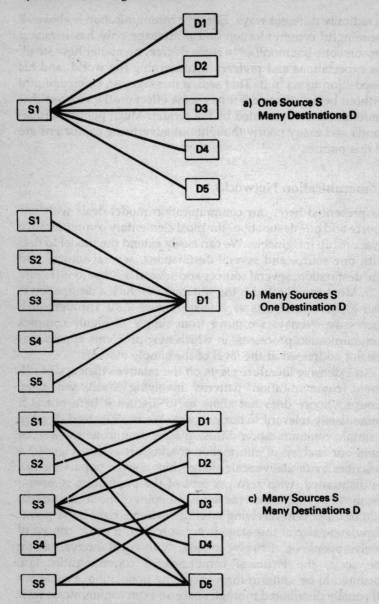

Figure 2.2 *Communication Networks.*

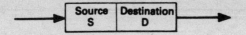

Figure 2.3 *The Relay.*

so on. This, of course, is a little artificial since in real life some choose to be hermits living in solitude in mountain retreats while others press against each other in high density urban slums. No matter; we are dealing with an abstraction.

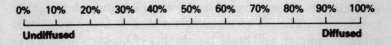

Figure 2.4 *A Diffusion Scale showing the Percentage of a Given Population receiving a Message.*

Broadcasting

We can now depict a variety of communications situations by positioning sources (which we shall label S) and destinations (which we shall label D) at different points of the scale. For example, by placing our Ss on the extreme left hand point of the scale and our Ds on the extreme right, we describe a communication structure that calls for *broadcasting* (Figure 2.5). In its most basic form, this is the teacher in the classroom. It is not efficient for him to lock himself up in his study and call his students in one by one to give each in turn a lecture on organic chemistry. No. He gathers them all in one room and speaks once. If his audience is too large to fit into a classroom he may use a large amphitheatre but then he might need to use a microphone in order to be heard at the back of the hall. With an even larger audience, he may have to broadcast his lecture by radio. But broadcasting, as we have just defined it, is not limited to the spoken word. The diffusion of textbooks or newspapers can also be considered as forms of broadcasting.

Note that the larger his audience, the less the opportunity for feedback. In the classroom, the teacher can take – and indeed

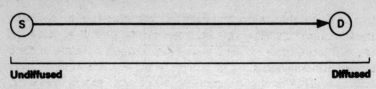

Figure 2.5 *Broadcasting on the Diffusion Scale.*

often welcomes – interruptions from students who need clarification. He can switch from a broadcasting mode to a dialogue according to circumstances. In the amphitheatre, on the other hand, the teacher is more constrained. Too many questions, asked at random, will break the rhythm of his presentation. He is best advised to defer questions to the end of his lecture. But with a radio talk, the pure broadcasting situation, no switch of mode is possible. If there is feedback, it will come from people who write in at their leisure with questions which the lecturer may or may not choose to answer – also at leisure.

Note also that in the classroom the teacher can use gestures, diagrams, and facial expressions to reinforce his message. So can his audience. If students in the front row are nodding off after fifteen minutes, the teacher can modify his message accordingly – at the extreme he can burst into song, tears, or flames. In the pure broadcasting mode, such immediate – if painful – feedback is not available. People can switch off their sets but this will not change what the broadcaster says or how he says it. He might be given his ratings, but hardly during his talk.

Scanning

If we now reverse the pattern and place the Ss on the extreme right of the diffusion scale and the Ds on the extreme left, we get a *scanning* process in which many sources address messages to a single destination (Figure 2.6). If they all speak with one voice, D will get the message loud and clear. If they speak with different voices, however, the result could be Babel. This is the principle of democracy. The greater the distance between the

Ss and Ds on the scale when used in a scanning mode, the lower the likelihood that any one message can be or will be attended to. A filtering process which ranks messages in terms of their potential relevance must be set up to make a scanning process effective. This is the function of a communication hierarchy which sets up a series of relay stations between a base which is rich in information, albeit of a highly fragmented and diversified nature, and an apex which can build up a total picture from the data provided by the base, but only if it has learnt to filter out the 'noise' from the information it requires as it moves through the relay stations on the way up the pyramid.

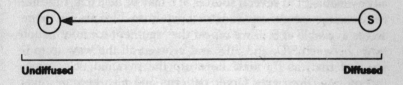

Figure 2.6 *Scanning on the Diffusion Scale.*

A communication hierarchy can be represented as a sequence of S/D points on the diffusion scale bracketed by one S point and a D point at each end (Figure 2.7). If we switch our attention for a moment from the communication structure itself to the way it distributes information along the scale, we can observe some interesting things. We shall make the assumption that the hierarchy described in Figure 2.7 describes an organization – it could be commercial, religious, or whatever – and that information, being valuable, is shared with peers and superiors in the hierarchy but not with subordinates. This is not always the way things work out since in many organizations one will be fairly selective about what one tells the boss so that not all relevant information flows upward, yet it is not an inaccurate description of the way information flows in most organizations. Perhaps one's peers in some circumstances receive more information than in others and in most organizations subordinates also receive information, albeit selectively, but we shall ignore such complications for the time being.

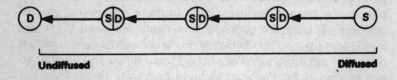

Figure 2.7 *A Communication Hierarchy in the Scanning Mode.*

Following this principle, we can easily see that information available at S is also available at S/D, *but that the reverse is not necessarily true.* S/D, by a skilful scanning of information generally available from several sources at S may be able to synthesize the data it possesses and construct patterns which are not themselves available at S. If we repeat the argument for information flows between S/D, and S/D^2 and proceed all the way up to D we find that, as the data flows up the pyramid, it becomes incorporated into ever larger patterns and also becomes ever more proprietary – that is, subject to retention. For example, a chief executive, acting on a review of the comparative performance of all product divisions, may decide to sell either the best or the worst performer. But he can keep this news to himself until the very last minute and thus maintain his options intact.

Of course, as just mentioned, information also flows down a communication pyramid, but in a discretionary manner. If I am obliged to tell my boss what I am doing with my time, he, conversely, is not obliged to tell me where he disappears to during those long lunch hours. I am visible to him where he can remain opaque to me.

Information as Power

The different points on the diffusion scale, then, are asymmetric with respect to their possession of information. The *volume* of data may be greater on the right and generally available to all, the *value* of information will be higher on the left and generally available to a select few. The distribution of information along the scale expresses power relationships based on the differential possession of knowledge. Those who know more in some sense have power over those who know less. Although knowledge has always been recognized as an important source of power, it is not the only one. A face can launch a thousand ships and sovereign princes can be made to dance to the tune of their creditors, yet knowledge as power has some strange properties not attributable to these other forms.

For a start, it is much more easily dissipated. Where knowledge can be reproduced – i.e. set down on paper – the marginal cost of doing so has become almost negligible. Consider for a second the difference in cost between cracking the genetic code and photocopying it once cracked. Knowledge that can be so easily reproduced and diffused can travel rapidly from left to right along the scale and quickly loses its proprietary value. Hierarchy may form a barrier to over-rapid diffusion but other barriers, such as patents, copyright, and so on, may also be needed to slow down the process.

But to block the diffusion of knowledge altogether may also be counterproductive. Knowledge that is hoarded cannot always easily be put to use so that sooner or later it has to be shared. To know how to turn base metal into gold is handy but not of much use if it requires a skilled team of chemists to whom you steadfastly refuse to divulge your secrets. The issue is not a trivial one. Copernicus kept his work on the heliocentric theory locked up in a drawer for nearly thirty years before consenting to have it published. He feared ridicule and persecution by the ecclesiastical authorities of the day – he was, after all, a canon – and only received a copy of the first edition of *de revolutionibus orbis* when he was lying on his deathbed.[3] The world today might be a very different place if the good canon had decided to keep what he knew to himself and Ptolemy's geocentric model still shaped our conception of the universe and our place in it. The great skill, then, is to share your knowledge in such a way as to increase your power rather than diminish it – it boils down to four simple precepts: *what* to tell; *how much* to tell; *whom* to tell; *when* to tell.

From Coding to Codification

To summarize, the structure of communication patterns will affect the way that knowledge is distributed along the diffusion scale of Figure 2.4, and hence will influence the development of power relationship within a given population. The picture is a very partial one, particularly in a complex society where individuals belong to different social groupings and organizations, and may therefore appear at one point of the diffusion scale in some situations and at a quite different point later on. Our simple scheme is not yet able to deal with such complexities; nor need it. There is one complexity, however, that we must deal with if we are to progress, and that concerns the level of coding of communications along the diffusion scale. We have so far treated the communication structure as if it were an autonomous variable, set independently of the communication process itself. In fact, as we shall see later, the way we code our messages and the structure through which we then push them, exert a strong reciprocal influence on each other.

But I must from now on stop using the term *coding*. It is very much an engineering term, altogether too cognitive and lacking in any sociological flavour. After all, we are not interested solely with what goes on within one mind, but with what goes on between them and, as we have said, if the structuring and sharing of information is the collective enterprise through which culture is built up, then the term *codification* will suit us better. One codifies social practice and experience – laws, the highway code, established custom, and so on. Codification, then, is only reduced to coding in the limiting case, when the experience being structured is to be found within one mind alone, an occurrence that we can assign to the extreme left hand corner of our diffusion scale.

What our analysis of codification in Chapter One now allows us to assert here is that the diffusibility of *uncodified* experience is much more problematic than that of codified experience and that fact imposes a number of important constraints on the structure of the communication situation. Its inherent ambiguity requires a higher level of redundancy and possibly several channels working together to reinforce each other. For example, when I meet someone for the first time, I am a bundle of correlations seeking to make a good impression. My facial expressions, my bodily movements, my utterances, must all work consistently towards the same end. Also my clothes – those subtle and misleading purveyors of image – must not undermine the message that I am trying to get across. An impression is a finely tuned orchestration of features that is hard to codify. If I know you well, I may be able to tell from your stoop and colour that you are depressed or unwell. If I meet you for the first time, the symptoms may escape me altogether.

Sharing Versus Transmitting Experience

Where experience is uncodified, then, a shared familiarity with context helps to transmit and diffuse it. But building up such shared familiarity takes time – sometimes years – and must be reckoned with when assessing the overall cost of communicating. How many things are left unsaid, not because they are unsayable but because the cost of doing so far outstrips the worth of the utterance? By explaining a joke, for example, one destroys its punchline and its effect. It thus becomes not worth explaining. However, below a certain level of codification, experience cannot be transmitted at all, it can only be shared. I can watch you ride a bicycle and I can then try to imitate you, but you cannot set out on paper how to proceed and assume that it will suffice.

A further complication with uncodified communication is that its lack of structure leaves much room for personal motivation, attitude, and belief to fill in the gap in interpretation. Quite often, a prior sharing of context or experience will not of itself suffice to get a fuzzy message across. There must also be some sharing of values to ensure that the communicating parties are on the same wavelength. This explains the initiation rites imposed by some followers of esoteric cults and practices who face the danger that their worldview will be challenged from within by deviants who have shared the experience with them and then choose to interpret it their own way. Shared values are the cement that bind together our partial and fragmented experiences, setting them into a coherent pattern.

The sharing of uncodified experience, in sum, requires a level of familiarity and trust between communicating parties that can usually only be built up in or around a face-to-face situation. Once built up, this stock of familiarity and trust might be extended to cover somewhat more distant friends, relatives, or possibly work colleagues, but it is quickly amortized – there is simply not enough of each of us available to cover all the interpersonal situations we may wish to participate in – and therefore must be used sparingly and with discrimination. In a word, uncodified communication is a slow business. How different is the case of codified communication which, with a suitable choice of transmitters and receivers, can spread through a population in seconds. Any movement in the price of ICI's shares can be known in New York and Singapore a few seconds after it is known in London. More important, an individual selling his ICI shares in London need never meet the buyer in Singapore. They communicate anonymously in a highly codified environment where share movements act as signals to which they respond. But even in what appears to be a more face-to-face transaction the codification needs that underlie the exchange will impose their own logic. Take as an illustration the following dialogue in a tobacconist's shop:

'Good morning.'

'Good morning, what can I do for you?'

'A packet of Marlboros, please.'

'I'm afraid we've run out. Will Stuyvesant do?'

'How much for 20?'

'£1.48.'

'I'll take them. Here you are.'

'Thank you.'

'Thank you. Good day.'

The dialogue is impersonal, highly focused, and could occur between any one tobacconist and any one customer anywhere, and at any time. Buyer and seller do not have to know each other, like each other, or trust each other. Cigarettes and money change hands simultaneously and no risk is incurred by either party. Of course, the customer could be a neighbour, have his children at the same school as the tobacconist, or go to the same pub. This could lead to a more diffuse transaction in which not only are extraneous personal elements introduced but a higher level of trust is correspondingly required:

'Can I pay you later?'

'You can buy me a drink tonight instead.'

'I'll do that anyway but I'll send Cathy in to pay you on the way back from school.'

'No rush.'

'Bye now.'

Thus the transaction, as it incorporates more elements and draws upon a wider breadth of shared experience from the parties, becomes less codified. It also changes its scope since credit now appears to express a change in the nature of the relationship between buyer and seller; each now requires prior knowledge of the other, more trust, and interpersonal involvement over a longer duration.

Yet even this second encounter crystallizes around well codified and diffused elements of information. The price of a packet of cigarettes is usually well known, as is the quality of the brand. There is little opportunity for dissembling or misrepresentation. If the quality of the transaction in some circumstances is enriched by extraneous elements its underlying basis remains the same. The next person to enter the tobacconists may be a total stranger just passing through and may not be able to buy cigarettes on credit, but he will still expect to get his Marlboros in the same quantity and for the same price as anyone else.

Conclusion

The relative difference in the ease with which codified and uncodified information diffuse in a population lies at the core of what follows next. It has underlain much of cultural anthropology, albeit in a more implicit intuitive form, and it will form the main subject of management anthropology as we shall construct it. The task of the next chapter will be to articulate the relationship between the codification and diffusion of knowledge and information into a number of theoretical propositions whose social – and, in our case, more specifically managerial – implications can be developed and explored. Our first two chapters, by clarifying the sense in which we shall be using the terms 'information structuring' and 'information sharing', have laid the groundwork for what follows.

References
1. Shannon, C., and Weaver, W., *The Mathematical Theory of Communication*, Urbana: The University of Illinois Press, 1949.
2. See, for example, Raven, B., *A Bibliography of Publications Relative to the Small Group*, Los Angeles, 1959.
3. A highly readable account of the development of the Heliocentric theory is offered in Koestler, A., *The Sleepwalkers: A History of Man's Changing Vision of the Universe*, Middlesex: Penguin Books, 1964.

Codification and Diffusion: C-D Theory

Introduction

This chapter is the most abstract in the book. It is not, however, particularly mathematical and will be accessible to anyone who can read a graph and who has not forgotten his high school algebra. For those readers who are not theoretically inclined but who do not wish to lose the thread of the argument, a simple one page summary of what is covered here is given in an appendix at the end of the chapter. The ideas presented in it are, of course, capable of further mathematical elaboration thus possibly enhancing their elegance and unintelligibility for the general reader. Science usually proceeds in reverse order, first presenting a few laconic equations to a restricted community of initiates, and then, when the commanding intellectual heights have been secured, descending into the valleys in search of popular acclaim through some less demanding 'popularization'. Yet some concepts can serve without elaborate and recondite formalization. They can be presented 'in the raw' at a fairly general level with some indication of the areas in which they might be of use and, if persuasive, they will invite further development whether mathematical or otherwise. This will be the case with what we shall term C-D Theory, a shorthand for Codification-Diffusion Theory. Although it has by now found its way into a number of professional journals, it makes little appeal as such to specialized knowledge or training and can therefore be judged by the educated layman no less than by the professional.

In fact, one of the most frequent reactions observed to the core propositions of C-D theory is frustration. 'It seems so obvious,' people comment, 'and yet no one seems to have taken the trouble of saying it.' Indeed, if you assert in a general way that information set down on paper diffuses more rapidly than information which is not, who will disagree with you? After all, was this not what Gutenberg was all about – the spread of books, the subsequent rise of an educated bourgeoisie? The very obviousness of the proposition seems to make its further codification superfluous, if not pedantic. Yet without some further structuring its implications escape one altogether.

Karl Popper, the philosopher of science,[1] has argued that a hypothesis, in order to be interesting, has to be improbable. In other words, it must have some information content that violates one's expectations. To say to you that, if you gaze out of your cottage window, you will see trees swaying in the breeze is an intrinsically less interesting statement than to say that you will see hot molten lava flowing towards you. The latter condition is less likely and thus less expected. To point it out is to be informative. The crucial test for C-D theory, therefore, is not whether its key concepts are in themselves hugely original but whether they give rise to hypotheses which, though initially improbable, turn out to be promising. In other words, does C-D theory have explanatory power or, to paraphrase the Heineken beer advertisement, does it refresh parts that other theories cannot reach? We shall examine this issue in later chapters. Here we must confine our attention to a simple presentation of C-D theory itself.

C-D Theory: The Reachable Audience

If, as has already been argued, the codification and diffusion of information are related, then perhaps a good point of departure for our analysis would be to bring together into a single representation the two scales presented in Chapter One and Chapter Two. Figure 3.1 presents a two-dimensional space created by using our codification scale as the vertical axis and our diffusion scale as the horizontal one.

To briefly recapitulate how these scales were created: the codification scale measures the extent to which a message is compressed into a code with compression ranging between 0 and 1, computed as the reciprocal of the number of bits of information required to formulate a message (i.e. $C = \frac{1}{n\,\text{bits}}$). At 0 no message compression and hence no coding can take place; at 1 the message can be compressed into a single bit. The diffusion scale measures the percentage of a population – also expressed as a co-efficient ranging between 0 and 1 – in possession of a given item of information. On the extreme left no one has it, on the extreme right everybody does.

The population selected for the purpose of the analysis can be quite varied. It ranges from a small group, to a firm, to an industry or even a nation state. Provided that the members of such a population are in some kind of potential or actual communicative relationship with each other – i.e. that for some purpose or other they form an interest group – then the propositions of C-D theory will apply to them.

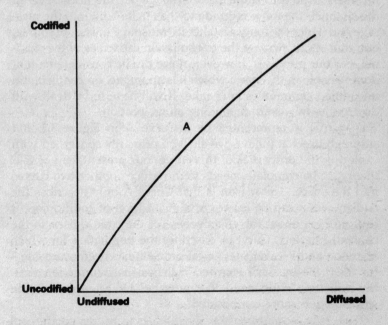

Figure 3.1 *The Audience that Can Be Reached with the Codification and Diffusion of Information.*

Our central proposition then is that the percentage of a target population that can be reached over a fixed period of time varies positively with the level of codification, i.e.

$$D = f(C)$$

where D is the rate of diffusion per unit of time measured along the horizontal scale and C is the level of codification measured along the vertical scale. f is some function that defines the specific shape of the diffusion curve for a given distribution of the population, communication technology, and so on. We shall not be concerned with elaborating this function although our later discussion will deal informally with a number of variables that it could incorporate. Nor shall we deal explicitly with the problem of noise in the communication process which is clearly inversely related to diffusibility. The higher the noise level in the channel, the more redundancy has to be built into the message and hence the longer it takes to transmit – unless, of course, one chooses to increase the transmission capacities of the channel. For our purposes, however, noise can be considered a random variable in the space which has an impact on codified and uncodified communications alike. It will have to be dealt with differently, however, depending on its location.

$D = f(C)$ is represented by a Curve A in Figure 3.1 and although in what follows we shall be primarily concerned with exploring the properties of this curve, our presentation of C-D theory, to be complete, needs to introduce another two curves into the space. The reason is that Curve A only describes the audience that can be *reached* at a given level of codification; it says nothing about the effectiveness of the code chosen in the context. In effect, Curve A describes the population for which Shannon and Weaver's technical problem has been overcome – for them the message received matches the information sent. But will they understand the message? Or act upon it? The situation gets more complicated.

C-D Theory: The Competent Audience

Curve B in Figure 3.2 defines the population *competent* to understand a message at a given level of coding. It suggests that the competent audience is inversely related to the level of coding. Why? Codes, like languages, have to be learnt and require a considerable investment in time and effort to master. They make for easy transmission but will only solve Shannon and Weaver's semantic problem if all communicating parties happen to share the same codes. If one of the parties has not made the necessary investment, if he needs to translate a message into his own codes using a dictionary or an interpreter, then the rate of diffusion drops, sometimes to a trickle. Take as an example the attitude of many westerners towards technical innovation in Japan. Ever since the end of World War II, so the argument runs, the Japanese have been assiduously absorbing western – and particularly American – technology by a careful perusal of English language scientific and technical journals. They pick up the technology, improve it and use it to compete with western firms both in their own and in third markets yet, in terms of innovations, they give little in return. Thus, until a few years ago, the Japanese were seen as imitators who took western knowledge but gave nothing. Yet how do we know what Japanese technical publications actually have to offer? How many governments or enterprises invest in the systematic translation of Japanese scientific publications to the extent that the Japanese have done with English language ones? The Japanese willingness to invest in language coding skills has allowed a massive diffusion of foreign technology into Japan. Conversely, the reluctance of foreigners to learn Japanese has effectively prevented whatever technological and scientific know-how that may exist to diffuse out of Japan.

Curve B argues that the lower the coding level of a message, the less prior investment in shared codes is required, and hence the greater the probability that any two people will be capable of understanding each other. Simply stated, more people are able to understand the meaning of a smile or laughter, of a wink and a nudge, than are able to speak Thai, or Spanish, and again,

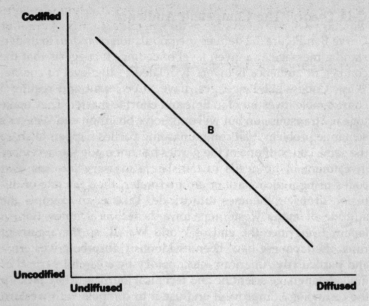

Figure 3.2 *The Competent Audience.*

in turn, more people are likely to understand a text in Spanish for a given level of effort than one in advanced mathematics. Yet such a generalization has to be stated with care since Curve B does not, like Curve A, describe the invariable technical properties of information but the variable properties of receivers. If, for example, governments everywhere decided to teach advanced computer programming to all children under the age of fifteen, one would surely see a considerable change in the shape of the curve. It reflects social practices as well as a principle of least effort, an attempt to minimize the expenditure of energy involved in the act of communication. Applied to the lower part of Curve B, the principle of least effort requires a sharing of experiences and a minimal use of codes; applied to the upper part, it requires a sharing of codes either as a complement to, or a substitute for a sharing of experience. Yet the basic point remains that the investment generally required to master a computer code is greater than that required to master the language of winks and nods. For the foreseeable future, a skilful flirtation will rely on the use of the eye rather than on a printout.

C-D Theory: The Interested Audience

What about Shannon and Weaver's effectiveness problem?

Understanding a message does not necessarily lead to an appropriate response. A receiver must be potentially *interested* in the message as well as capable of understanding it. Telling my elder daughter that it is very late will not get her out of bed on a Sunday. Telling her that bacon, sausage and egg is waiting and getting cold will transform the somnolent hulk into an anxious goal-seeking glutton. Thus a destination may receive and understand a message but still fail to act on it. The message is not meaningless in a semantic sense – he could explain the message to you if required to – but it is meaningless *to him* given the pattern of his concern at the time he receives it.

Generally speaking, though, the degree of codification of a message does not per se affect the size of the audience for whom it has potential meaning. The medium may be the message as McLuhan has told us but it is not the message's meaning. We can therefore draw a Curve C representing the interested audience as a vertical line in the diagram (Figure 3.3) indicating that the size of the relevant audience is unaffected by the form given to a message. Of course this vertical line is nothing other than the one by means of which one distinguishes an interest group from other possible groupings. It thus helps to create a specific diffusion space. Once it has been created, the portion of the space that lies to the right of the vertical line shown in Figure 3.3 can, for most purposes, be discarded. Defining the interested audience is typically something that is done at the beginning of the analysis. In some cases the exercise is straightforward and follows the institutional lines through which we carve up the world: the British architectural profession thus constitutes an interested audience for some purposes, just as ICI does for others.

Communication Strategies

By bringing the three curves together, we obtain a summary graphic description of the role played by codification in Shannon and Weaver's three communication problems. We are, of course, dealing with communications in the aggregate and, as in many models, we leave much of the real world out of account but, by playing around with these three curves a bit, we can get an intuitive feel for what might be involved in formulating an effective *communication strategy*.

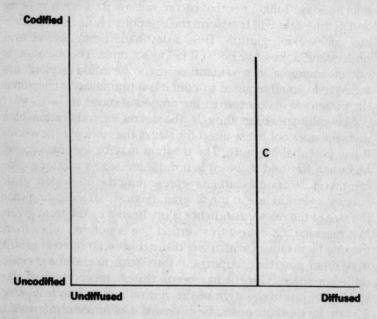

Figure 3.3 *The Interested Audience.*

If we take the term communication strategy to mean the efficient allocation of scarce resources to achieve given communication objectives, then the optimal strategy available can only be had at that point in the space – assuming it exists – where the three curves A, B, C intersect *and* coincide with a target audience, represented by a vertical line T in the space

(Figure 3.4 gives an interesting example). The target audience may exceed the size of the interested audience, or it may be much smaller. In the first case one may talk of *proselytizing* strategies; in the second, of *esoteric* strategies.

At any other point in the space than the one where the three curves intersect, additional resources will need to be expended and this in one of three ways:

- To develop a communication infrastructure which allows the physical transmission of messages at different levels of codification, and therefore either allows movements up or down and across the space along Curve A, or brings about a change in the shape of Curve A itself. Here one is addressing Shannon and Weaver's technical problem.

- To develop a common coding system at different levels of codification that allow a vertical and horizontal movement along Curve B or, again, a change in the shape of the curve. Here, one is addressing Shannon and Weaver's semantic problem.

- To develop a shared set of values and beliefs that will change the location of Curve C along the horizontal scale and hence the size of the audience – by either expanding or shrinking it – for whom the message has potential meaning. Here, one is addressing Shannon and Weaver's effectiveness problem.

Codification and diffusion, then, define a two-dimensional *culture space* (which we shall henceforth abbreviate to C-space) in which the existing social distribution of knowledge and individual communication strategies interact in specifiable ways. The existing distribution of knowledge expresses past communication strategies, and acts as a constraint on the formulation of new ones. It can be considered as the product of a cumulative social investment in communication infrastructure, coding skills, and social values which, at the margin, sets the costs of the various strategic options available to the individual communicator. Of course, effective communication strategies in turn redistribute social knowledge in the C-space. Effectiveness here

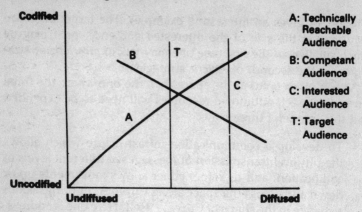

Figure 3.4 *The Target Audience.*

depends on developing some intuitive feel for the shape of the three curves in the C-space. Otherwise stated, it requires a fair degree of familiarity with a given culture, whether it be national, corporate, professional, or whatever.

A Typology of Knowledge

The three curves that we have described act as hidden forces that push knowledge and information hither and thither in the C-space – an epistemological pinball machine in perpetual motion. At different points, the space exhibits specific properties that partly reflect how these forces exert their influence in that region. To examine these properties more closely, let us artificially simplify things by reducing our codification and diffusion scales to two categories each that we might define as follows:

Scale 1: *Codified –* information that can easily be set out on paper for transmission

Uncodified – information that cannot easily be set out on paper for transmission

Scale 2: *Diffused –* information that is readily shared

Undiffused – information that is not readily shared.

Using this dichotomized version of codification and diffusion, we might produce the typology of knowledge shown in Figure 3.5. The diagram does not tell us whether the knowledge depicted resides within one brain or within several. It could represent what is known by a single individual but it could just as well refer to a firm or a wider social grouping as we shall see in more detail in Chapters Five and Six. In fact, although we shall not elaborate on the point here, Figure 3.5, when used organizationally, provides us with the link we seek between cultural anthropology and management. For now, however, we shall confine our discussion to the typology itself. How was it arrived at? Let us take each element in turn:

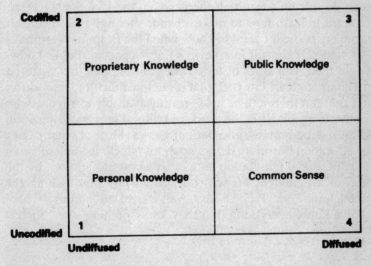

Figure 3.5 *A Typology of Knowledge.*

Public Knowledge

Codified and diffused, this is the kind of knowledge that accumulates in textbooks, scientific journals, magazines, libraries and public archives. More specialized variants also exist in the shape of statistical year books, trade publications, financial records and so on. Public knowledge is generally available and subject to checking and scrutiny from many sources giving it a self-correcting character. Yet because most of it is transmitted impersonally, some control is sometimes exercised over its authentication. If I learnt that $E = MC^2$, it was not because Albert Einstein took me aside for a ten minute session of confidential revelations, but because I read it – albeit with some reluctance – in my physics textbook at school; and since school textbooks are considered to be authoritative sources of uncontroversial knowledge, I could risk investing time in learning the formula without running the risk of being duped.

Also, for most purposes, public knowledge is sufficient. If I want to find out how American industrial shares are performing, I can do this by consulting the pages of the *Wall Street Journal*; if I want to learn how to make a lemon meringue pie, I consult a cookery book; if I want to know when the Peace of Westphalia was signed, I consult Everyman's Encyclopaedia. Public knowledge, then, is a stock of tested facts and figures that is stored at a comparatively low cost, that is not too difficult to reproduce, and that can therefore be made readily available to anyone who wishes to use it. It is the stock in trade of crossword puzzles, TV quiz programmes, and parlour games. Most of what passes for education in society draws upon this stock. Its limitations as an educational foundation are perhaps best brought out by the quip of an eminent French statesman who, after visiting the prestigious *École Polytechnique*, was heard to mutter, 'These people know everything, but they know nothing else.' Such is the nature of public knowledge.

Proprietary Knowledge

Where knowledge has been codified but not yet diffused, it has a scarcity value over and above its reproduction costs, which people will pay for. Those who possess proprietary knowledge can thus trade it for other benefits, whether these be money, prestige, authority, or influence. The term proprietary here describes more than just patentable technical knowledge: a share tip, a mathematical formula, the monthly financial report of a regional subsidiary, all of these have a proprietary quality that can be exploited for varying lengths of time. Yet since such knowledge is codified, it is inherently diffusable and, unless the audience competent to understand it is exiguous, those who do not possess it exert pressure on those who do. Resisting such pressures means erecting barriers to the diffusion process in order to control who gets access to the information, and on what terms. Thus, for example, certain types of financial information in an organization are typically only available at a certain level of the hierarchy and very often what comes out of a firm's corporate research laboratories is only for the eyes of top management. In fact, the higher you move up the organizational pyramid, the more proprietary (still in the wider sense of the term) the information used tends to become, whether it deals with a firm's product-market strategy or its contingency plans for dealing with a strike by plant maintenance engineers.

Unlike public knowledge, which can be scrutinized by all, proprietary knowledge is often hard to evaluate by potential recipients. How much is it worth paying for a share tip? For patent information? Who else has this information been given to and how can one find out? Have I been told everything or is my informant economizing on the truth? And so on. Although such questions pose difficulties that in economics fall under the heading of 'moral hazards' or 'adverse selection',[2] as a rule they are not insuperable. Enforceable contracts can be written, safeguard clauses devised, and some contingencies anticipated, all of which minimize the knowledge recipient's risks. Such is not the case where the knowledge in question is uncodified.

Personal Knowledge

Where an individual's perceptions and insights have not been given a structure, where they resolve themselves into formless and fleeting intuitions that escape all attempts at recording and storing them, we get what the philosopher, Michael Polanyi, has termed personal knowledge.[3] Hazy recollections of early childhood days, a familiar yet elusive fragrance, intimate moments with a friend or a loved one, perhaps these form the bulk of our everyday experiences and act as an unconscious substratum upon which our articulate knowledge must ultimately rest.

Personal knowledge, then, is neither codified nor diffused. It cannot be stored, examined or evaluated either by its possessor or those around him to whom it is made manifest. As such, it can only be intuitively apprehended, and thus has value primarily for its possessor. But, as Polanyi himself has cogently argued, it is no less knowledge for that. You may not be able to explain just what it was that allowed you to recognize someone that you have not seen for twenty years as he passed you in the street but if you call out his name he will either respond or he will not. Thus your knowledge of him will turn out to be valid or invalid, even though tacit. Personal knowledge must not be confused with subjective knowledge which cannot be subjected to external testing.

In a number of cases, rare to be sure, personal knowledge has a universal value. The vision of a Cézanne – *ce n'est qu'un oeil, mais quel oeil!*: in this case personal and subjective knowledge intermingle – contemplating the Mont Saint Victoire, or the intuition of an Alexander Fleming in translating the accidental glance at a laboratory culture into penicillin, both attest to the power of personal knowledge.[4] Yet, being uncodified and hence largely untransmissible, such knowledge cannot be traded *whilst in that form*. It remains inalienably the property of the brain in which it originates. Others may be invited to share the experiences that give rise to personal knowledge but different intuitions and perceptions will then result.

And sharing such experiences, as C-D theory tells us, is the slowest and most time-consuming of all diffusion mechanisms. It may take many years for the Zen novice to achieve his master's proficiency and even then nothing guarantees that he will succeed. In fact, it may be a condition of his success that he learns to trust the master and accepts his authority on very personal and uncertain grounds. It is in such intangibles that charismatic power resides. It is a power that can ellicit supreme effort and sacrifice among disciples, and can also be much abused, leading in the worst cases to tragedies like the one at Waco in Texas or in milder cases to convinced millenarians sitting on mountain tops patiently to await the second coming. Personal knowledge, for good or ill, is also personal power.

Common Sense

The greatest protection against the abuse of charismatic power is a healthy endowment of common sense. Knowledge, uncodified yet widely diffused, may sound like a contradiction of the key proposition of C-D theory that relates diffusion to codification, but it is nothing of the kind. Common sense is not acquired by reading the morning papers or the weather reports. It is built up very slowly through a process of *socialization*, the intangible product of a lifetime of personal encounters at home, at school, at work, and in the streets. Common sense is what everybody knows goes without saying. It harbours archaic custom and folk wisdom no less than an intuitive knowledge of when and how to cross the road. Common sense, more than any other kind of knowledge tends to take the world for granted as it finds it.[5] Why else do we shake hands, raise our glasses, and eat our pudding at the end rather than at the beginning of the meal? Common sense thus diffuses slowly and by osmosis through the limited network of personal relationships by means of which we acquire our sense of personal identity. As with Personal Knowledge, a lack of codification injects ambiguity into transactions involving the transmission of common sense, and the resulting risks and uncertainties can only be counterbalanced by a certain level of interpersonal trust between the parties and, hence, a minimum sharing of core values. Such trust is not given freely to the man in the street, to the anonymous stranger, but is built up slowly through personal contact so that it may be readily available to those with whom we are most intimately concerned – parents, spouse or children – and then, more conditionally, to friends, professional colleagues, neighbours, and other stable elements of our social landscape.

The key point about this kind of knowledge is that being a common possession implicitly held, it creates a shared context that minimizes the need for redundant communications. It is unnecessary to dot *i*s and cross *t*s, and a word or two will often suffice to get your meaning across. It draws upon what the sociolinguist, Basil Bernstein, in another context, has termed a 'restricted code',[6] a jargon or set of shorthand expressions that are generally the property of a small group. Thus while common sense, by definition, is shared knowledge, its writ often does not run very far beyond the small group or groups in which it originates. This has been forcibly brought home to me living in Beijing over a period of time when the car population has almost tripled; from a few solitary cars that had to wind their way past oblivious pedestrians, to long queues of idling engines waiting patiently upon the caprice of the traffic policeman to zoom off, Beijing has become a much more dangerous place for both pedestrians and cyclists. Yet the road sense that we unconsciously take for granted in the west given our long familiarity with town traffic, is almost entirely absent there. It is not that the average Chinese pedestrian or cyclist is more stupid than his counterpart elsewhere, but that his total lack of any prior encounter with the motor car until recently has prevented him from developing that intuitive behavioural repertoire that tells him where to look when he crosses the street, when to stop or when to proceed. The outcome is a city that can rival Paris in the number of road casualties turned in each year, at one hundredth of the number of vehicles per head of population. What is common sense to the Parisian is not evidently so to the Beijinger.

To summarize, common sense, like paint, to be spread widely must be spread thinly. Much of it can only diffuse locally and within a restricted radius, and any attempt to share it universally produces fissures and cracking that reveal basic social groupings and divisions. Where common sense appears to be universal, it is usually because a similarity in local conditions has produced a similarity in local responses. What might pass off as sound practice to an Indian peasant could well appeal to a Mexican one faced with similar tasks.

Conclusion

The knowledge typology just presented does not claim to be exhaustive but it does illustrate the links that exist between an information environment, the nature of the social relationships that build it up, and the kind of social knowledge that results. However, the picture we have drawn lacks dynamism. Social knowledge may be classified by our typology but it is not trapped by it. If C-D theory says anything at all, it says that at times t_2 knowledge is not where it was at t_1; it flows through the C-space with torrential rush in some places and at the sedate pace of a glacier in others. At one level of resolution, C-D theory can say little about such movements, for their complexity and variety defy description, but if we step back a little, a pattern emerges that is of potential interest to an emergent information society. The pattern at present is in the eye of the beholder and retains the character of an untested hypothesis. But it is neither implausible nor untestable and, having important implications for the creation of a managerial anthropology, it will be presented in the next chapter.

Appendix: C-D Theory – A Recapitulative Summary

The extent to which knowledge and information diffuse through a given population is directly related to how far it has been compressed or codified. Yet although technically speaking more people can be reached by more codified messages, more training may be required to master the codes so that in effect fewer people may understand them. The sender of a message, in formulating his *communication strategy*, must take into account those opposing tendencies as well as the size of the audience he is trying to reach. As a rule of thumb, one could say that the lower the level of coding the more likely that communications will be confined to face-to-face situations and that, with increasing codification, larger and larger audiences can be reached by impersonal means. Nevertheless, the *volume* of information that can effectively be transmitted at any coding level will depend on the de-coding skills of the receiver.

The two dimensions of codification and diffusion create a *culture space* (C-space) in which communication strategies may be studied. These produce different types of knowledge such as:

- *Public knowledge* such as textbooks and newspapers, which is codified and diffused.

- *Proprietary knowledge* such as patents and official secrets, which is codified but not diffused. Here barriers to diffusion have to be set up.

- *Personal knowledge*, such as biographical knowledge, which is neither codified nor diffused.

- *Common sense* – i.e. what 'everybody knows', which is not codified but widely diffused.

Knowledge is not static in the C-space but is constantly being redistributed from one quadrant to another. The next chapter explores how.

References
1. Popper, K., *The Logic of Scientific Discovery*, London: Hutchinson, 1959.
2. Moral hazard and adverse selection are discussed in Eggertsson, T., *Economic Behaviour and Institutions*, Cambridge: Cambridge University Press, 1990.
3. Polanyi, op.cit.
4. Macfarlane, G., *Alexander Fleming: The Man and the Myth*, Oxford: Oxford University Press, 1985.
5. Schutz, A., *The Phenomenology of the Social World*, London: Heinemann, 1972.
6. Bernstein, B., *Class, Codes, and Control: Theoretical Studies Towards a Sociology of Language*, Vol. 1, London: Routledge and Kegan Paul, 1971.

Knowledge Cycles

Introduction

It is not knowledge that flows in the C-space but the information on which it feeds, and it moves at a pace and in patterns dictated by the influences exerted respectively by our three curves. Knowledge is what builds up in the minds of individual receivers in ways that are usually only marginally affected by information flows at a given moment. Prior stored knowledge has a much more important role to play since it orients the receiver towards one set of messages rather than another and sets the degree to which he will be receptive or indifferent. To somewhat overstate the case, few people other than astronomers are well placed by dint of prior training to tune in to intergalactic radio signals to find out what is going on. Yet stored knowledge is ultimately shaped by the cumulative effects of external information flows interacting with existing mental structures to produce stratified layers of experience, some of which are readily accessible, others less so. So there is a sense in which knowledge as well as information can be said to move in the C-space. The aim of this chapter is to examine this movement and, although we shall start with information flows, the patterns through which knowledge emerges and is socially shared will be our main concern.

Movement in the C-Space

At any point in the C-space, a number of forces are at work which can be resolved into four vectors as in Figure 4.1:

- Upward towards greater codification

- Downward towards less codification

- Rightward towards more diffusion

- Leftward towards less diffusion

Yet, unlike vectors describing mechanical forces, these do not cancel each other out when they are of equal strength. You can move towards more and less codification at the same time, and more and less diffusion, but you might move faster or more decidedly in one direction than another. To illustrate, a flow left towards less diffusion may represent a manager's monthly report to his superior further up the organization pyramid – he will, in turn, retransmit upwards – and the flow to the right towards greater diffusion might represent the same information going to his subordinates. The boss gets a thirty-page report of financial facts and figures, whereas subordinates – say a factory workforce – get a three paragraph summary in the company magazine. Or, again, take a company board meeting. If an agenda marks out an intended communication activity for the group, then the 'informal' interpersonal horse trading and politicking that may take place before and during the meeting represent a move towards less codification since most of it will be 'off the record', whereas the minutes of the same meeting, a pithy and uncontroversial selection from what actually took place, take us towards greater codification – one communication format for insiders; another for outsiders! But even a vectorial thrust in one direction of the C-space may have several components. A thirty-page publication in a scientific journal, for example, may enjoy a limited diffusion within the scientific community but a much wider diffusion in the popular press when summed up as a ten inch column article. Both acts of communication may operate at the same level of codification – not all scientific reports invoke arcane mathematics – but the jargon used in the scientific report may restrict its diffusion to a limited audience competent to understand the code. The press article has filtered out this jargon but only by carrying out a drastic dilution of the initial message. Its gist may remain so that the main point may be grasped by the lay reader but its richness has been drained away.

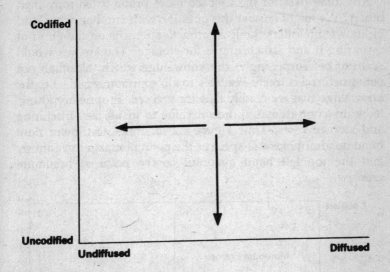

Figure 4.1 *Vectors in the C-Space.*

Entropy in the C-Space

The vectoral movements described, then, irrigate the C-space with information. If it falls on fertile soil, knowledge will grow at that spot even if much information just runs off. Yet just as healthy plants grow and die, so do the minds that store knowledge. Even if information is externally stored in libraries or archives it is subject to the action of time. Records are destroyed, lost, or simply thrown away; the codes required to make sense of them are no longer available – who today can read cuneiform script?; people cease to be receptive to the messages they contain. In other words, the knowledge that builds up in the different parts of the C-space is subject to the action of *forgetting*, that gradual process of erosion that in physics goes under the name of *entropy*. The term describes a process of destructuring and disorganization to which the whole of the physical universe, if conceived of as a closed system, is subjected. Seen in this light, absent-minded professors are just a taste of greater things to come!

Are some parts of the C-space more prone to entropy than others? We might answer this question with another: what kind of knowledge offers the least attractive returns on the effort of capturing it and structuring it for storage? The answer would seem to be, surprisingly, the knowledge which, although not yet structured is freely available to all, common sense – i.e. the knowledge that we readily take for granted. Proprietary knowledge by contrast has sufficient value to justify its structuring and storage costs. Thus Figure 4.2 identifies the lower right hand quadrant of the C-space as the point of maximum entropy and the top left hand quadrant as the point of minimum entropy.

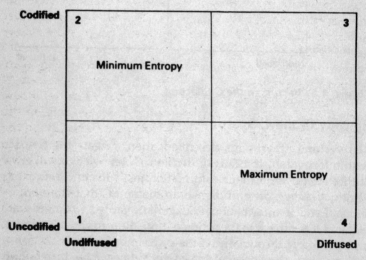

Figure 4.2 *Entropy in the C-Space.*

Communication strategies we have earlier defined as the allocation of scarce resources to communicative ends. Communication strategies, then, must reckon with the action of entropy in the C-space. Although it may act with greater force in some regions, it is pervasive. How many people today know how to produce a Gothic thirteenth century illuminated manuscript?

How many would be capable of performing ancient Egyptian burial rites? Not many, one might reasonably suppose; yet both of these skills in their day were prescribed and recorded in great detail. Some of these records, to be sure, still exist but for us they have degenerated into mere information having long ago ceased to be knowledge. As communication strategies the records in which the information is stored have ceased to be effective. They gather dust in museums and libraries and await the occasional consultation. Entropy has taken its toll at the technical, semantic, and effectiveness levels; our three curves, here, have become pale shadows of their former selves: few audiences can be reached; fewer are competent to decode; fewer still are interested.

But it should not be assumed that all communication strategies necessarily aim to counteract the action of entropy. After all, there are things that individually or collectively we would prefer to forget. Our descendants may not thank us for the resulting loss of potentially valuable information but, where memories are painful, time exerts a healing effect that attenuates the intensity with which we recall events, reducing them by and by to scarcely discernible contours emptied of feeling. Thus do we see a new generation of young Germans grow up that will never know the Second World War as their parents did. Those who lament the inability of humanity to learn the lessons of history sometimes tend to underestimate the extent to which old learning can block new learning. (See Bob Garratt's book in this series, *The Learning Organization* for more on this.) Forgetting is too often seen as a tragic predicament that condemns humanity to the treadmill of past errors; these perpetuate themselves as cycles of suffering or wheels of misfortune running towards an indefinite horizon. Yet forgetting is also an essential step in the metabolism of experience; as such it needs to be regulated rather than overcome.

Creating New Knowledge in the C-Space

Regulating the metabolism of experience by taking into account the dynamic properties of information in the C-space is what communication strategies are all about. At any point in the space, knowledge can either be built up, maintained or reduced by a suitable allocation of communication resources. If entropy broadly describes the process by which knowledge is reduced, how is it built up? At a simple level, the answer seems to be by investing in the creating, storing, transmission or reception of information at particular points in the space. Yet such an answer is really too simple for it tells us nothing about the *patterns* such investments could or should adopt or about how these patterns exploit or counter the dynamic properties of information flows in the C-space. In short, what we still require to know is in what ways such investment patterns can be said to amount to a *strategy*.

To answer the question satisfactorily, we first need to go back to the information flows themselves. If these were totally random then a strategic allocation of communicative resources would probably be impossible to achieve. Particular acts of communication, to be sure, may be improved on, but in a haphazard episodic way which would not allow a cumulative investment. The random action of communicative forces would set in motion information flows that would threaten to sweep away whatever had been built up. This is no way to encourage strategic investment. We shall argue that, whereas for our purposes most information flows in the space can be treated as random, the creation of *new* knowledge exhibits an identifiable pattern and that an understanding of how this particular pattern is created is relevant to the formulation of strategy. Although it is difficult to test for, the pattern is easy to describe and can be illustrated with everyday examples.

The Four Phases of a Knowledge Cycle

New knowledge is created when the actions of our four vectors resolve themselves into a clockwise flow in the C-space as represented schematically in Figure 4.3. Each vector represents a distinct phase in the build up of new knowledge that we can label:

1 Scanning (S)
2 Problem Solving (P)
3 Diffusion (D), and
4 Absorption (A)

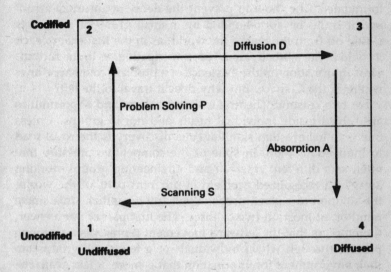

Figure 4.3 *The Cyclical Flow of New Knowledge in the C-Space.*

We shall now briefly describe each of these phases in turn.

Scanning (S)

The creation of knowledge is usually the outcome of a response to a perceived problem or opportunity. These could be of any kind – technical, scientific, social, political, financial, and so on – and the knowledge created is not necessarily directly related to the problem treated. It often happens, for example, that scientific knowledge is produced when seeking a solution to a technical problem – this has typified much innovation in the chemical and pharmaceutical industry in both the nineteenth and twentieth centuries – or that, inversely, technical knowledge results from a search for solutions to a scientific problem – the development of the telescope and much scientific instrumentation being a case in point.

The problem could be well codified – i.e. increasing the packing density of electronic circuitry on a silicon chip – or scarcely formulated – i.e. how to prevent the decay of an urban area – and it could be apprehended by a small group of specialists closed off from the rest of the world, as in the first example, or it could invite a broad, grass root participation, as in the second. Thus information on the existence of a problem could arise anywhere in the C-space. But why does it travel to the left?

For two reasons. The first is that problems and opportunities are solved inside individual heads and not in groups. Unless one is to believe that simultaneous discovery is the royal road to innovation, then, in spite of the competitive pressure that often sets different research and engineering groups working away at a recognized problem in different parts of the world, the solution to a given problem will emerge initially in a single mind or, at most, in two or three. The first part of our answer, therefore, is that the leftward movement represents a scanning process through which individuals or a few small groups tap their environment for information that is more or less available, more or less shared, and more or less codified.

But, it might be argued, surely what is registered by individuals located on the right of the C-space is also lodged in individual minds. If these individuals scan their information environment, no leftward movement will necessarily result. Perfectly true, but what the leftward movement tells us is that, although a problem or an opportunity may be there for all to see, we do not all perceive it in the same way and that it requires a highly singular perception to frame a problem in such a way as to produce new knowledge in solving it. In other words, those who experience the problem usually form a larger class than those who address it actively and these, in turn, in the case of new knowledge, outnumber those who can solve it innovatively. Thus the second and most important reason that our scanning activity points leftwards in the C-space is that only one or two minds possess the singularity of vision to convert a shared problem into new knowledge. And if the *data* concerning a problem or opportunity are shared by many, the ways that these data get configured into unique or singular *visions* are not. It is here that personal knowledge, perishable as it is, asserts its worth, not as a capricious flight of fancy but as an idiosyncratic way of knowing that involves the whole being. Singular vision is often deviant vision. The social pressure to conform, not only in what one does or says but also in what one thinks or feels, usually acts to stifle the development of such vision or its expression; hence its appearance in the least populated region of the C-space – on the left.

Problem Solving (P)

Identifying the solution to a problem usually means exploring alternative possibilities and making choices between them. Some will be eliminated, others will be further explored in detail through the creation of sub-alternatives and the making of further choices. The process is a bit like 'twenty questions' in which one tries to successively narrow down an answer by first asking very general questions – is it animal, vegetable or mineral? – and gradually homing in on specifics – is the melting point lower than 27 degrees Celsius? In effect, codification and problem solving are the same thing – both seek to give a structure to experience. Our problem solving vector therefore describes an upward movement in the C-space.

Where problem solving occurs on the left, as in the diagram, it is a highly personal skill which, in the lower regions of the space, is impossible to specify. In some rare souls it might go under the name of genius. In more common cases it is what we call creativity. Yet even these cases are not really so common. Often, what passes for creativity is merely inventiveness – the ability to generate novel combinations which only superficially address a problem. Genuine creative problem solving is often a risky business. Some alternatives have to be selected – the essence of codification – under highly uncertain conditions, and, by implication, some have to be rejected. The process of choosing often leads to conflicts where different members of a group or a community have invested emotionally in rejected alternatives. Because it is so personal, the emotional stakes can be very high, and more often than not – in fact in the great majority of cases – the search process leads up blind alleys. 'Ten per cent inspiration, ninety per cent perspiration', as George Bernard Shaw put it. Only a certain kind of temperament can stomach the risks and uncertainties involved, a temperament which perhaps does not register the hazards as others do but, having sometimes an unshakeable faith in its own personal vision, may come to see a particular line of enquiry as potentially fruitful where others, perhaps more easily influenced by the assessments of their peers, would have long ago abandoned it as hopeless.

With increasing codification, however, both problems and solutions become better defined and can therefore embed themselves more easily in the existing stock of knowledge. X, a new item of knowledge, then becomes an instance of Y, an established item of knowledge, for which known procedures and solutions exist. Thus as one moves up the C-space, problem solving becomes less *heuristic* and more *algorithmic*, that is, the process evolves from one in which problem solving procedures cannot be specified and outcomes cannot be guaranteed towards one in which both can be. The risks and uncertainties of course are, by this stage, much reduced and the payoffs are clearer, so that a larger number of people may now be willing to invest time and effort in working in the problem area. Thus, with increased codification of possible solutions to the problem, we get increased diffusion, at first through face-to-face encounters, and then gradually through other channels – publications, radio, products, and so on.

Diffusion (D)

Very little problem solving is carried out in total seclusion. Even intimate, personal problems are usually discussed with friends, relatives, or work colleagues, so that diffusion takes place, albeit interpersonally and on a small scale, with the very first attempts at codification. Unless an explicit effort is made to block diffusion, Curve A in Figure 3.1 (p. 61) is a more accurate description of the diffusion pattern than the more schematic representation of Figure 4.3 (p. 83). With increasing codification, new audiences become reachable: a scientist, for example, will communicate verbally with his work colleagues, through an internal document within his organization, through a brief research report with the scientific community, and through press articles with the general public.

Yet moving from one target audience to another can be a delicate matter. If knowledge has value to the message source, then its diffusion must be carefully controlled. In giving details of a patent, for instance, you must describe your contrivance in sufficient detail to prevent would-be competitors from 'inventing around' you, yet you must avoid setting down on paper those little tricks of the trade that are known only to you as the inventor and developer of the device and which actually form a large part of your protection. Thus you codify some things for your work colleagues and other things for a larger audience.

It may seem paradoxical, considering the potential value of new knowledge, but the need to control its diffusion will be felt by recipients no less than by sources. After all, if it is genuinely new, it is not as yet extensively tested. So how can one be sure that it is valid? The public is easily duped by authoritative pronouncements. The man in the white coat with the stethoscope hanging down his chest can probably get you to swallow a nasty looking brown liquid more easily than can your street corner grocer. The banker who sits in his spacious oak-panelled office is more likely to talk an ageing widow into switching her savings into municipal bonds than a share tipster who accosts her in the street. And how many of us, when shopping in a supermarket, remain wholly indifferent to the claim that toothpaste X is recommended by dentists because it contains .03% of Methyloglocyn (a word, I hasten to confess, that I have just invented)?

Yes, the unsuspecting public definitely needs protecting from quacks, charlatans, and the ravages of misinformation. But then *who* will do the protecting and on what grounds? As a rule, politicians, who plead for a responsible press and complain that they have been misrepresented to the public by hostile media, more often than not are concerned to secure protection for themselves rather than conferring it on their constituents. 'More open government' is usually the cry of opposition parties, not those in power. Censorship, then, is a double-edged sword that, by placing control of the diffusion process in a few hands, gives them great power. The expression 'knowledge is power', in effect, can be read in two ways:

1 power to put that knowledge to use – for example, building a refinery

2 power over those who do not possess that knowledge – for example, knowledge by an 'insider' of a takeover bid on the stockmarket.

The two overlap, sometimes reinforcing, sometimes contradicting each other. You cannot build a refinery on your own and therefore you need to share most of your knowledge with others if you are to achieve your goals. But, in the case of the imminent takeover, your power to use your 'insider' knowledge disappears if others possess it, too. You must be able to buy into the target company while the share price is low. If others, also having insider knowledge, drive up the share price by their purchases, you have lost your information advantage.

The first kind of power is distributed throughout the C-space and is roughly proportional to prior investments in knowledge. The second kind of power is purely relational and therefore increases as one moves towards the left in the C-space where it has scarcity value. New knowledge emerging on the left of the space thus initially confers a power on its possessors that gradually drains away as it diffuses towards the right and loses its monopolistic attributes. The more codified the knowledge, the faster the potential diffusion rate and the greater the tendency to set up barriers that will allow those who have it to hold on to it.

Absorption (A)

For a message to be effective it must change a recipient's disposition to think or act – i.e. it must have an impact on the structure of his expectations. A message does not come and encrust itself like a barnacle on existing knowledge structures. It penetrates and modifies them, for the most part imperceptibly, but at times in important ways, its ripples being felt throughout the structure. The more intensive and extensive the ripples, the more 'meaningful' the message is said to be.

The rippling effect results from attempts to integrate and reconcile newly received information with existing knowledge. Darwin's theory of natural selection, for example, could not be reconciled readily with the then prevailing biblical account of the creation. If his central message were to be accepted, then major adjustments in cosmological thinking would be called for and, indeed, perhaps even in the value system of knowledge recipients. Yet, once such a process is under way, even a very simple codified message can work its way into a person's unconscious through the force of repetition and practice, and come to affect the way he sees the world. Such a process of information absorption is described by a downward movement in the C-space towards those regions where knowledge has once more become implicit, uncodified and, for the most part, unconsciously held.

But, of course, the type of knowledge possessed by recipients will vary with their position on the diffusion scale; and so will the messages they receive. A biologist, for instance, reading about the synthesis of insulin in *Nature* is neither getting the same message as the reader of a *Times* science report on the subject, nor is he reacting in the same way. A downward vector placed on the left of the C-space, where we might place our biologist, simply does not produce the same kind of uncodified knowledge as a downward vector placed on the right, where our *Times* reader resides, so that the absorption process produces a social partitioning of the C-space that reflects the differential possession of knowledge by different social groups.

The integration of new and existing knowledge is not only

an intellectual process. It is brought about by putting the new knowledge to use in situations that have often not been anticipated by its creator. This 'learning by doing' in effect constitutes an extensive test of the new knowledge's validity and scope and the downward movement of the absorption process taking place on the right of the C-space is continuously modifying it and blending it to suit local requirements. Could Denis Gabor, for example, the inventor of the hologram, ever have anticipated its development as jewellery?

There will be times when new and old knowledge cannot be reconciled, when they either choose to ignore each other – for example, the particle versus wave theories of matter – or they are condemned to a uncomfortable coexistence. Such failures can serve as triggers for a new knowledge cycle in which attempts to eradicate the anomalies give rise to fresh acts of codification on the left of the C-space.

A failure of absorption could occur at any point during the course of downward movement. In the upper regions of the space where existing knowledge structures are well codified, the anomaly is clear and visible, referring perhaps to a contradiction or an inconsistency that has to be dealt with.

In the lower regions, things are more complicated. For a start, learning by doing is a slow business carried out by numerous small cells and, by the time the problem is spotted and acknowledged as such, much integration in the upper regions may already have taken place, thus increasing the level of social commitment to the new knowledge. Second, an anomaly in the lower region, where so much is implicit, may be hard to interpret, sometimes being nothing more than a vague feeling of discomfort that things are not what they should be. Finally, since messages in the lower region travel so much more slowly than in the upper one, triggering off a new knowledge cycle will be a much more difficult and time-consuming business than where messages and knowledge are well codified. In sum, the social responsiveness to problems arising in the uncodified regions of the C-space will be less than where these are well defined.

Different Kinds of Knowledge Cycle

The knowledge cycle we have described is an idealized one. Having a large perimeter in the C-space, it stands for the creation of radically new knowledge which leaves no part of the space unaffected. It also takes the longest time to complete. The very slow movement of uncodified information at the bottom of the C-space can be measured in years and often in decades. Other cycles are possible, expressing different communication conditions. Prior investments in knowledge, social discontinuities along the diffusion scale, and innumerable obstacles to thinking – i.e. discontinuities in the codification dimension – and communicating, all conspire to create a wide variety of cyclical patterns as in Figure 4.4. The various cycles of Figure 4.4 will run at different speeds so that the flat cycle A at the top of the diagram will operate much faster than the tall cycle on the left. All will be clockwise, however, where they involve the creation of new knowledge.

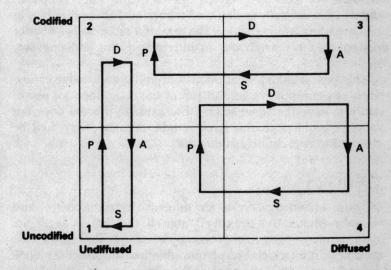

Figure 4.4 *Different Cyclical Patterns in the C-Space.*

Barriers to the completion of a knowledge cycle abound in the space. The scanning process may never achieve the leftward movement necessary to achieve a singular and original perception of a problem since social pressures may stifle the deviant perception. Problem solving may shun the risks and conflicts incurred in selecting and eliminating alternative options, for codification is a risky business that involves negation as well as affirmation. Diffusion may be blocked by censorship or by an unreceptive audience; the visionary is condemned to being misunderstood and sometimes to being persecuted. Finally, the downward movement of absorption may stall as new knowledge butts up against the inertia of existing values and attitudes. The barriers may destroy the cycle, slow it down, or deform it; understanding how they operate is an important part of understanding the behaviour of knowledge cycles.

As individuals, we participate in several knowledge cycles that reflect the diversity of our social involvements and at times we may act as a link between them – being recipients of knowledge in some instances and producers in others. A top flight scientist, for example, may be one of two or three people in the world who really understand monoclonal antibodies but, in reading his morning paper at the breakfast table, he is no better placed than his neighbour in interpreting the parliamentary news.

This brings us to a final point concerning knowledge cycles. Each one is unique: a second run of the cycle does not necessarily involve the same actors; the scanning process does not lodge a problem in the same minds; diffusion may well be directed to entirely new audiences.

Conclusion

In sum, knowledge cycles are difficult things to control and manage. Should one even try? After all, they are an aggregate description of exceedingly complex information flows, the greater part of which escape our attention altogether let alone our understanding. Are we not then being too ambitious?

My answer is that organizations and institutions are social

attempts to manage information flows and that an understanding of knowledge cycles and how they work can only improve their performance. By placing the cycles in a C-space, we affirm the cultural dimensions of knowledge creation; we also establish a link between the cultural strategies through which knowledge is structured and shared, and the effectiveness with which institutions and organizations are managed. As we shall see in the next chapter, the C-space defines an information environment for the development of social conduct. Communication strategies are expressed through transactions that vary in scope and structure from one part of the space to another. A specification of these transactions will complete our theoretical work; it will also be the last step in the road we have been travelling from the world of cultural anthropology to the world of management.

5

Transactional Strategies

Introduction

How people relate to each other will partly turn on what they can talk about and how. Just as a successful marriage is not built around a telex machine, so the most genuinely competitive bid for the construction of an oil refinery is unlikely to be submitted by a close relative of the chairman of the firm calling the tender. Looked at in the C-space, communications are characterized by:

- increasing uncertainty as one moves down the space. Uncodified communications are ambiguous and, partly for that reason, are very slow to transmit.

- an increasing relative power of the message source as one moves leftward in the space, where useful knowledge becomes scarce.

How do these simple facts affect communicative relationships? And is there, then, a link between the various types of knowledge that we have identified in various parts of the C-space and the kind of transactions that are possible in that region? After all, transactions, taken there in the sense of any encounter between two or more people that involves some form of exchange, are the building blocks of human relationships, and presumably transactions must be guided by information relevant to their purpose if they are to be successful. At the most basic level, even something as simple as an exchange of greetings requires:

- Recognition of an actor as someone known to us

- Information, through gestures or smiles, that one's proffered greeting will be favourably received

- Knowledge of the appropriate alternative forms that a greeting should take. When does a 'Hi!' sound too familiar, or a 'It is a pleasure to meet you' too pompous?

- Some estimation of what follow-through the transaction will require. Remember that in some cultures, the question, 'How do you do?' can elicit an alarmingly detailed and time-consuming reply!

Much of this we know unconsciously, which is why we would classify a simple greeting as largely uncodified even though the various forms that it can take will often be found to spread over several pages of a standard book of etiquette. But how many of us ever rely on books of etiquette in the conduct of our social relationships? If you work for a public relations firm and regularly pair up prelates and film stars at charity balls then a book of etiquette might indeed prevent you from committing social blunders but, when it comes to dealing with your mother or your work colleagues, you would cut a strange figure consulting such a document in order to avoid giving offence!

Transactions, then, are complex social events that must now be incorporated into our analysis. Perhaps a good starting point for our discussion of transactions is our visit to the tobacconist described in Chapter Three. What can we say about the information environment or about the social relationships that characterize the exchanges that occur when purchasing a packet of cigarettes?

Markets

The first point to make is that the transaction draws heavily on *public knowledge* that is both well codified and diffused. A packet of Marlboros is understood to contain twenty cigarettes of a certain quality and length. Many purchasers will not even talk about the price as it is already well known through advertising or prior purchasing from competitors. The tobacconist will possibly hand over the packet without a word, take the money and give the right change without commenting. A perfunctory thank you may follow but if it does not the purchaser may not even notice.

Thus the second point is that the transaction is usually quite *impersonal*. As suggested in Chapter Three, the degree of personalization may vary but is not essential to the transaction. The purchaser may be a hardened criminal on the run or a Nobel prize winner for physics, he will still get his packet of Marlboros. The tobacconist may be a Trotskyist or regularly beat his four-year-old daughter – it is all the same to the buyer. Clearly, the transaction is *more* likely to take place in certain cases where such biographical information is *not* diffused and available to the other party. The key point here is that the transacting parties do not have to share common interests, values, or beliefs in order to do business.

The third point, then, is that each party is free to *pursue its own interests* and goals in the transaction. The vendor earns his living by selling as many cigarettes as he can, the purchaser finds his salvation in purchasing as many cigarettes as he thinks he needs. The tobacconist may disapprove of people who smoke. But who cares? Each individual has enough information available to him to decide for himself what he wants out of the transaction. The area in which the respective objectives of buyer and seller converge is the one in which he can do business. The rest is irrelevant. Caveat emptor.

The final point to be made is that the availability of information to all makes the system largely *self regulating*. Should the tobacconist wish to raise his price, he must reckon with the strong possibility that the customer will go elsewhere. Should the latter try to haggle over the price, he knows that the vendor can find other customers who will trade at the going price. The self regulating character of the system is due to the large number of tobacconists and cigarette buyers who can readily act as substitutes for each other and who are then driven to adjust their own behaviour accordingly.

What we have just described of course is a classic *market* transaction under conditions of perfect information. As economists have long told us, market transactions, to be efficient, require that information on price, quantity, and quality be widely distributed to both buyers and sellers. Other conditions such as ease of entry into the market and the divisibility of goods on offer also influence efficiency but this need not detain us. Our concern is simply to note that the information environment of a pure market transaction requires the codification and diffusion of relevant transactional data.

Bureaucracies

For the next type of transaction we shall discuss, let us follow the purchaser of the cigarette packet when he leaves the tobacconist and let us assume that he returns to his office. He has just finished his lunch break. During his absence, a number of documents have piled up on his desk and await his signature. One of them is marked 'Confidential' and turns out to be a spending request by one of his subordinates working in a branch office of the organization in a neighbouring town. The request is set out in a standard format as required by the company's investment department and has a number of supporting documents attached. These turn out to be insufficient, so a number of files and additional documents must be consulted before a decision can be made. Perhaps the proposed expenditure must be compared with competing alternatives; or again it must be evaluated in the light of the organization's development policy, and so on. So what can we say concerning this transaction?

First, much of the information on which the decision will finally be made, although set out on paper and kept in files and therefore well codified, is not generally available either within or outside the firm and therefore it is not widely diffused. We are therefore dealing with a form of *proprietary knowledge*. The subordinate will not know on what grounds the decision was made because much of the information is not available at his level of the hierarchy.

Second, it is perfectly conceivable that this particular decision maker has never met this subordinate so that the relationship is, in effect, an *impersonal* one. The decision will rest on the merit of the case and will be taken on rational grounds that will (or should) ignore the identity of the petitioner. Certain formal procedures will have to be followed in order to arrive at a defensible conclusion, calling for a certain number of skills and prior training – say in financial analysis or marketing – that the current incumbent is deemed to possess. Thus, in contrast to a market transaction, neither party is free to pursue its own personal objectives but is constrained to serve a well defined 'higher' organizational purpose with rationality and impartiality. Yet, as with a market transaction, the parties are not required to share common values, beliefs, and attitudes beyond those just mentioned, to wit, rationality and impartiality. They may both enjoy golfing and turn out to be fanatical chess players, or one may be a Sunday sky diver and the other an amateur snake charmer. No matter. The decision will be made in total disregard of such personal niceties. After all, it may have to be submitted to the cold scrutiny of a higher authority.

The fact that superior and subordinate share a common and well defined organizational purpose allows the first to *delegate* a certain decision making authority to the second in the knowledge that, providing he is given the requisite information and possesses the relevant skill, he can be trusted to take the same decision that his superior would have taken in his place. Thus a controlled and highly selective diffusion of information, usually performed on a strictly 'need to know' basis, is the key to effective delegation of hierarchical authority. To illustrate: below a certain sum of money, the subordinate may be free to make the spending decision himself, but he should then he prepared to defend it on substantially the same information grounds that were used when referring the decision upwards.

With increasing delegation comes the need for a *hierarchical co-ordination* of the work of subordinates. Where they encounter problems in their work that do not fall within the provision of the organizational rules prescribed, they pass the problems up the hierarchy to the level at which the rules can be modified or, if needs be, discarded. But this means that, as one moves up a hierarchy, the rules available to decision makers reduce in number, and the information environment in which decisions are made becomes less and less codified. A firm, for example, may require a 15 per cent return on its new investments but how do you establish where you stand in relation to that hurdle when launching a technically new product in a new market? Does the risk premium asked for ever signify anything more than the tendency to quantify wishful thinking?

In spite of the lack of codification as one approaches the top of the organizational pyramid, the transaction that we have just described is typical of *bureaucracies*. Information is well codified but its diffusion is strictly regulated by the operation of a hierarchy. The pyramidal structure of an organizational hierarchy shows information flowing up – this could be regarded as something of a scanning motion – and also flowing down. It is clear that, while the base may hold on to some types of non-codified information and that not everything gets systematically reported to the boss, the top of the hierarchy, by piecing together the information fragments coming from the base, can build up a composite picture of an organization's activity which is not available at the base and which offers hierarchical superiors a strategic information advantage which can often be converted into power over subordinates.

Fiefs

Let us now leave our executive to his decision and shift our attention to another part of his organization. We might assume, for example, that he works for a large industrial firm with a sizeable Research and Development effort. As we enter one of the laboratories carrying out basic research, we meet a small group of scientists sitting around in a corner of the space and engaged in an intensive discussion. The team leader, a world class specialist in crystallography, is listening to the results of an experiment recently carried out by his laboratory colleagues. Transactionally speaking, what do we have?

The scientific knowledge used by the team leader in evaluating what his colleagues are telling him is in large part codified and there may be daunting quantities of it, but those critical knowledge elements that put him in a class of his own, and perhaps to which he owes his reputation, are *personal*. It is uncodified and reflects the slow accumulation and absorption of high quality idiosyncratic experience within a single brain. It is the fruit of a lifetime's investment in a particular branch of learning. Such knowledge, or 'know-how', as it is now called, cannot readily be described. It can be transmitted in a limited way to close colleagues by force of example as when, for instance, they participate with the team leader in setting up and conducting an experiment and, by observing and sharing directly in the experience, they pick up the little 'tricks of the trade' – the calibration of an instrument, the interpretation of a reading, and so on – that gradually contribute to their own stock of personal knowledge. Note however that it then becomes *their* personal knowledge and no longer that of their leader. Certain elements may be shared but for the most part such knowledge remains a singular possession.

For this kind of group to transact effectively it must be very cohesive. Its various members must 'get along'. Relationships are of necessity much more *personalized* than in the case of the bureaucratic transaction. The research team has been built up into a highly productive work group by their leader over a number of years. He is concerned to develop to the full the potentialities of the individual researchers. To do this well he must get to know each individually: his background, his aspirations, his strengths and weaknesses, and possibly his personal circumstances. The outcome is the kind of research team that the Nobel Laureate Enrico Fermi managed to develop in his Rome laboratory, a group of scientists who, as Gerald Holton[1] observes, 'had practically grown up together'.

The personalized relationship between team members is essential to the building up of a sense of shared values and trust between them, and essential to the very *personal authority* of the team leader. The power he wields over his team is of a very intangible kind. It does not essentially reside in his official position on the organization chart, nor on his ability to offer promotions or salary increases, but rather on professional ability and personal qualities. This is *charismatic authority*. It creates disciples rather than subordinates and its power to command obedience depends on the existence of personal loyalty based on trust and shared values rather than – as with bureaucratic authority – on the ability to coerce. The team and its leader may share the same scientific objectives but these may well be personal to the leader himself and express his own long term professional aspirations.[2] In industrial R and D, when it comes to choosing research projects, what is good for the individual researcher often turns out to be good for the corporation although some corporations might dispute this.

As in the case of a bureaucratic transaction, co-ordination will also be hierarchical although less so, and certainly less formally so. Team members will be 'on the same wavelength' and will co-ordinate their work according to a set of implicit norms that reduce the felt weight and the visibility of hierarchy.

The transactional style just outlined works best with small, highly dedicated groups. Charisma's writ does not usually run very far: its power is inversely proportional to distance, and it is only in the twentieth century, when the media have been able to diffuse selected features of the 'face to face' and the personal touch to a large population – think, for example, of President Roosevelt's 'fireside chat', or the Elvis fan club – that it has been able to extend its dominion. Yet, with distance, its effects are hard to sustain over the long term so that it is most effectively exercised with a small band of disciples – the New Testament seems to suggest that even twelve is one too many – with whom intimate personal contact can be maintained on a regular basis.

The word I have chosen to describe this type of transaction is the *fief*, a term that expresses the absolute yet circumscribed reach of personal power. If the word has accumulated more negative than positive connotations, it is because we tend to associate it with the abuses of personal power. Also personal power per se is granted little legitimacy in most circumstances and is redolent of a feudal order that in an industrialized society is considered the hallmark of corruption and underdevelopment. Yet a moment's reflection will show us that, where personal knowledge is of a quality that can translate into personal power, something like a fief will emerge. Fiefs abound all around us: in firms, on university campuses, inside the home.

Only in exceptional cases, however, do they enjoy any institutional legitimacy. Where they do, we can observe what Max Weber called the 'routinization of charisma',[3] a move over time from a fief to a bureaucracy, an attempt to inject some institutional stability in what is an inherently transient and unstable transactional form. In our analysis, we shall accept the somewhat feudal transaction characteristic of fiefs as constituent elements of the social order.

Clans

The last type of transaction that we wish to study still concerns our crystallographer. When his research team's work is completed, he will write up their findings in the form of a research report that he will present at the next meeting of his scientific association. This will be a pre-publication presentation through which he will solicit comments and criticism from his professional colleagues. His research findings will probably be put forward in an abbreviated form and couched in a professional jargon that implicitly assumes much prior shared knowledge among the participants. Yet what might therefore appear as *common sense* to a gathering of crystallographers may be somewhat inaccessible to the man in the street untutored in the arcane concepts and terminology of the discipline. Such jargon, however, allows an extensive use of 'restricted codes' in which much uncodified knowledge is shared with professional colleagues.

As with any professional association, relationships are built up through a network of *personal* contacts with one's peers, so that it is likely that our crystallographer will know a good number of those present at the meeting. Scientific meetings like this one are supportive events in which professional colleagues, through their presence and their behaviour, affirm their joint commitment to a common set of goals – i.e. the disinterested pursuit of scientific truth – and a *shared set of values*. Our scientist's findings may be criticized, but it will be done constructively and in the service of a joint cause. In some professions, shared values are articulated in a professional code of behaviour that practitioners undertake to observe. The code, however, is usually a loosely formulated set of general principles or moral maxims that are often difficult to enforce so that professional transactions still depend a good deal on the existence of trust between a practitioner and his colleagues or clients. As might be predicted from our earlier discussion, the more codified the skills required in a given profession, the lower the degree of trust required in a given transaction and the easier it becomes to write a contract for it. It is easier to sue an auditor for negligence than a neurosurgeon, and a neurosurgeon than a psychoanalyst.

The professional norms and values that regulate the behaviour of our crystallographer in relation to his professional association are not hierarchically imposed as in a bureaucracy or a fief. They evolve through a process of face-to-face *negotiations* among peers, in which politics and personal power may sometimes weigh more than rational deliberation. Where such interpersonal power is evenly distributed among participants, we may speak of a collegial process; but where it ends up concentrated in one or two hands we are, in effect, back in a fief. The resulting transactions themselves are also the outcome of negotiations, often conducted implicitly – a horizontal process akin to a market rather than a vertical bureaucratic one. Yet if it is a market it is a very inefficient one. The need for common values and the uncodified nature of the information shared by participants tends to limit the number of players to what can be handled in face-to-face relationships – oligopoly rather than pure competition; smoke-filled rooms rather than the trading floor. Entry is restricted and individual players are expected to observe the 'club rules' that serve to disguise the extent to which they pursue their own individual interest, and also impose upon them some minimum concern with the common weal. Such transactions are characteristic of *clans*.

Where entry is not restricted and the number of players increases, clans tend to break down. The uncodified norms and values that act as a social cement lose their power to bind. A good example of a clan structure breaking down today is offered by the City of London, where a rapid increase in the number of international financial institutions competing for business in what is rapidly becoming a global industry has led to an erosion of those uncodified City norms and values that can only find expression in the informal interpersonal network that had been the traditional strength of the 'Square Mile'. Aggressive competition by newcomers, some marching to the beat of quite a different drum, is slowly moving the City away from clan and towards market transactions. Thus, the much heralded 'Big Bang' of 27 October 1986, designed to do away with restrictive practices in Britain's financial markets, has merely been an inevitable – albeit big – step on the slow road from clans to markets.

Transactions in the C-Space

We can assign the transactions just described to the different regions of the C-space as in Figure 5.1. Their main characteristics are given in Table 5.1. As our own choice of examples indicates, in a complex society one would expect to find a mix of transactional styles reflecting a variety of information environments and social arrangements. Yet each expresses in its own sphere a set of beliefs about how the world should be ordered: if you hold that competition among gentlemen is unseemly then you will not feel comfortable in the market quadrant. Nor will you if you believe that those at the top of the social pyramid should govern those at the bottom with a firm hand, else chaos will ensue. Each quadrant in the C-space, then, can be associated with a *cosmology* that legitimizes the values and preferences of those who inhabit or seek to inhabit it. Yet, just as not everyone who waltzes into a tobacconist's subscribes to a free market philosophy, so not everyone who transacts out of a given quadrant shares its cosmological orientation.

In a simple society, a single cosmology, a single transactional style may predominate. In a complex society, several will co-exist side by side in pluralistic fashion. The cultural anthropologist, Mary Douglas, in her book *Natural Symbols* (1973)[1] and in later works, has explored the relationship between different cosmologies and the social order, but her cosmologies *create* the social order and do not result from it. Our own approach is

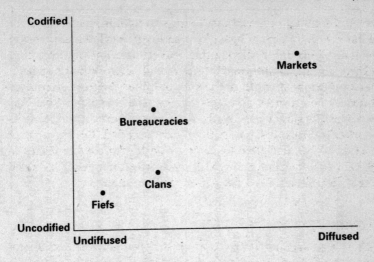

Figure 5.1 *Transactions in the C-Space.*

frankly more materialistic, although not dogmatically so. By analysing an information environment and the resultant transactional patterns that it gives rise to, we are looking at the circumstances that favour the emergence of a given cosmology. Once in existence, to be sure, a cosmology exerts its own influence upon events and may come to modify both transactional preferences and the information available. But a cosmology, in our view, is both an effect and a cause, interacting with transactions in an information environment.

A Digression on Materialism

If I may be allowed a theoretical digression at this point, the reciprocal relationships we have established between information, transactions, and cosmologies may help to place the old debate between idealism and materialism in a new light. Simply stated, idealism has stressed the impact that ideas have upon material conditions, and materialism has stressed the reverse, namely the importance of material conditions upon the evolution of ideas. Our analysis suggests that idealism and

Table 5.1 *Main Characteristics of the Transactions in the C-Space*

	Codified Information	Uncodified Information
Undiffused Information	**2 Bureaucracies** ■ Information diffusion limited and under central control ■ Relationships impersonal and hierarchical ■ Submission to subordinate goals ■ Hierarchical co-ordination ■ No necessity to share values and beliefs	**1 Fiefs** ■ Information diffusion limited by lack of codification to face-to-face relationships ■ Relationships personal and hierarchical (feudal/charismatic) ■ Submission to superordinate goals ■ Hierarchical co-ordination ■ Necessity to share values and beliefs
Diffused Information	**3 Markets** ■ Information widely diffused, no control ■ Relationships impersonal and competitive ■ No superordinate goals – each one for himself ■ Horizontal co-ordination through self-regulation ■ No necessity to share values and beliefs	**4 Clans** ■ Information is diffused but still limited by lack of codification to face-to-face relationships ■ Relationships personal but non-hierarchical ■ Goals are shared through a process of negotiation ■ Horizontal co-ordination through negotiation ■ Necessity to share values and beliefs

materialism are not mutually exclusive ways of seeing the world and may be part of a single movement, so that both may be a valid way of representing things at different moments.

Material conditions are not represented directly in the C-space, yet prior investments in knowledge and the costs of transacting in different parts of the space may be material conditions enough for our purpose. Prior investments create a transactional infrastructure that may favour one quadrant over another and may provide the stability required for institution building. Institutions lower the marginal costs of transacting in a given region of the C-space and hence act as a magnet for the uncommitted transaction, the one that has not yet been given its particular form. To take a specific example, inside an enterprise, the decision to fill a particular vacancy from within the firm's own ranks could take a bureaucratic form if the appointment is made purely from above, and a market form if the incumbent is recruited on a competitive basis by inviting suitably qualified staff to apply for the post. If the firm has already invested in time and procedures that favour the bureaucratic form, then the costs of switching to the market form will be correspondingly greater. The firm already possesses a transactional infrastructure that will bias its choices at the margin.

If such transactional infrastructures represent material condition, they do not do so in the traditional Marxist sense that refers to the physical means of production. Yet, interestingly, in an information society, one in which services will in future account for as much as half of Gross National Product, knowledge becomes the key productive factor so that the differential possession of information does in effect re-establish a link between an individual and the means of production, now newly defined. Institutions – the firm, the family, the professions, the market, and so on – become the channels through which transactions irrigate the C-space with information and knowledge. Where the soil on which they flow has been built up with prior investments in transactional infrastructures, the transaction is more likely to get soaked up and to bear fruit.

Yet the soil itself is always shifting under the pressures of these flows, and with altered topographical conditions new areas open up and old ones become barren. I am referring, of course, to the action of the knowledge cycle in the C-space which is constantly modifying our information environment and thereby redistributing our new 'means of production'. A mismatch then emerges in places between the existing institutional order with its established transactional biases and the new underlying 'material' conditions defined by the newly created information patterns. Marx called this the gap between the relations of production and the conditions of production.[5] The institutional order then either adjusts to the new reality and follows the cycle, or it digs in its heels in order to slow down or break the cycle. The whole thing is information driven, and sums up in a simple scheme the problem of institutional change.

The key point that emerges from our discussion is that transactions are the vehicle through which individuals, groups, or organizations express their communication strategies in the C-space. A transactional style is effective when it makes sense of the information environment and the existing or anticipated behaviour of the knowledge cycle. What has been presented here is purely conceptual and with suitable adaptations could be applied at the level of whole societies right down to that of individuals within them. Since our own chosen focus is managerial, we shall develop our analysis at an intermediate level, that of the firm. When one considers the astonishing variation in the size of what passes for firms – from, say, seven to seven hundred thousand people – this is hardly very constraining.

Conclusion

We have now completed our presentation of C-D theory at a general level. We must now sharpen our focus and come down to earth where firms struggle for control of markets, where production people snipe at marketing people, and where R and D remains aloof. In this jungle of organizational processes, does C-D theory have anything to offer? As presented so far, C-D theory is essentially concerned with the political economy of information. Political economy has always homed in on what a society has taken to be its critical resource. For the physiocrats still under the shadow of feudalism, the critical resource was land; for mercantilists in an age of discovery, it was gold and silver; in the industrial era, both labour and capital fought for primacy; and today, in an age of computers and global data networks, the critical resource has become information. Yet, in spite of a widespread intuitive understanding of this fact, we still lack a coherent political economy of information – emerging information technologies of themselves will not provide one. Surprisingly, the pressure for such a theoretical development has emerged from a stable normally far removed from any technical concerns with 'bits', packet switching, and modems: anthropology. How else can we account for the sudden appearance of a widespread concern with the 'soft' issues of culture at the very moment when we risk being submerged in a sea of data? The shelves of bookshops are overflowing with titles that are placing culture centre stage as an organizational and institutional issue. The reason, of course, should be clear to anyone who has followed the thread of the arguments presented so far: if cultural anthropology is about information structuring and sharing, then it is from this discipline that we may expect a political economy of information to emerge. C-D theory aims to be just one step along the road of its future development.

So, in concluding this first part of our book, our earlier question concerning cultural anthropology might be rephrased: does a political economy of information have anything to offer the practising manager and, if so, where does C-D theory fit in? The second half of the book attempts an answer.

References
1. Holton, G., *The Scientific Imagination*, Cambridge: Cambridge University Press, 1978.
2. Kidder, T., *The Soul of a New Machine*, New York: Avon Books, 1981.
3. Weber, M., *Economy and Society*, Berkeley: University of California Press, 1978.
4. Douglas, M., op.cit.
5. Marx, K., *Capital*, London: Lawrence and Wishart, 1887.

PART TWO

Applications

6

The Industrial Enterprise in the C-Space

Introduction

The sociologist, Kurt Lewin, once remarked that, 'there is nothing as practical as a good theory'. If, then, we want to know whether we have a good theory, we must now become a little more practical. The second half of the book is designed to bring us gently down to earth from the conceptual heights at which we have been orbiting. As we approach the ground, we must think of selecting a landing spot. What part of the planet do we want to explore? What, in fact, are we looking for and could we recognize it if we saw it? In the descent from abstract conceptualization to concrete reality, the choice of terrain is critical. To end up on top of a rocky crag from which one cannot get down, or to get lost in the desolation of desert sands, is just plain bad navigation.

Our choice of terrain will be the modern industrial corporation. It is fertile, offers a rich and varied topography and, if it is handled with care and talked to nicely, a moderately collaborative native population. Alternative habitats could also be studied in the C-space for it claims a general application: the scientific community, the professions, Trobriand Islanders, and the Reform Club, but, since one cannot land in several places at once without discomfort, a choice has to be made. In any event, we shall have the opportunity of making forays into neighbouring territories as the need arises so that we are not confined to one spot.

In this chapter, we shall lay the groundwork for an examination of the modern industrial enterprise in the C-space. We shall start by adapting the codification and diffusion dimensions developed earlier to the requirement of organizational analysis. Then we shall try to fit different parts of the firm, a bit like a jigsaw puzzle, in the C-space. Third, we shall examine what influence the cyclical flow of knowledge in the space exerts on organizational processes that go on within the firm. Finally, we shall consolidate whatever insights are gained by this work in order to have them readily available in subsequent chapters. Our approach will be commonsensical rather than scientifically rigorous, relying on the force of well chosen individual examples rather than the massed impact of carefully regimented statistical data. David rather than Goliath.

Codification and Diffusion in Practice

How do codification and diffusion translate into operational practice? What questions should one be asking of a firm's employee in order to assign the transactions he is involved in to one of the four quadrants – markets, bureaucracies, fiefs, and clans? A sophisticated and durable answer to these two questions would require substantial research and would probably lead to the construction of an index for each scale. Many features of a transaction, each with its own set of measures, would have to be incorporated in the index and then tested for validity, accuracy, robustness, and so on.

For most purposes, however, more rough and ready answers will do. Arguably, two simple questions could be put to a firm's employees that would take us a long way in understanding their information environment and its transactional implications:

1 Is the knowledge that you depend upon in transaction X set out on paper?

2 Is the knowledge that you depend upon in transaction X available outside your firm?

Answers to these simple questions will produce two dichotomized scales, the first describing the extent to which knowledge used in a given transaction has been formalized in documentary procedures, the second, the extent to which knowledge is specific to a given firm. Clearly, the first describes codification, the second diffusion.

Refinements to the two scales are possible. For example, one could trichotomize the codification scale by asking whether transactional knowledge is expressed mainly through gestures or verbally, through written words, or through numbers. Figure 6.1 illustrates such a scale. However, the scale conceals a trap for the unwary, for it might be assumed that more documents means more codification or formalization. Such a view accords well with our intuitive understanding of bureaucracy: more formal procedures as a rule mean more paperwork. But remember that codification is abstraction, the compression of information so that as you move from verbal to written embodiments of knowledge there may well be more paper involved, but as you then move from written words towards numbers and symbols there should in fact be *less*. There is thus a curvilinear relationship between the extent to which transactional knowledge is formalized and the amount of paper consumed. The paperless office of the 1990s, for instance, is a natural sequel to the mountains of computer printout of the 1970s, made possible by a *further* formalization of office procedures embodied in software. Perhaps, then, our trichotomized scale should be constructed according to whether transactional information is transmitted through face-to-face interaction, on paper, or via a computer.

Taking the diffusion scale, one could ask whether the knowledge required by a transaction was generally available to customers, to competitors, or even to other departments within the firm (see Figure 6.2). At the left hand extremity of the scale, one would end up with what an individual knows that no one else does, at the right hand extremity with what passes for universal knowledge. How people are then distributed along the scale depends both on the purpose for which the scale is used and on the structure of the relationships that one is investigating. Thus a variety of scales might be constructed for different purposes.

In effect, there is no single magical formula for translating the codification and diffusion dimensions that create the C-space

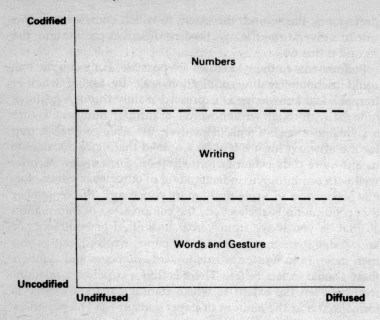

Figure 6.1 *Trichotomizing the Codification Scale.*

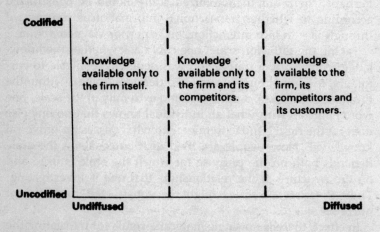

Figure 6.2 *Trichotomizing the Diffusion Scale.*

into an all-purpose set of empirical scales. C-spaces have to be tailor made to specific requirements and several fittings will be needed to achieve elegant effects. Our own immediate requirements are for a somewhat loose fitting dichotomized set of scales (Figure 6.3) which, taken with our earlier theoretical musing, yields the following proposition:

> 'The more knowledge relevant to a transaction has been formalized, the more easily it can be shared by different members of a firm, *and* the more accessible it is to outsiders.'

In other words, the line of least resistance for information flows is along the diagonal shown in the diagram, from quadrant 1 to quadrant 3. But this is none other than our codification and diffusion curve of Figure 3.1 (p. 61) in a new guise.

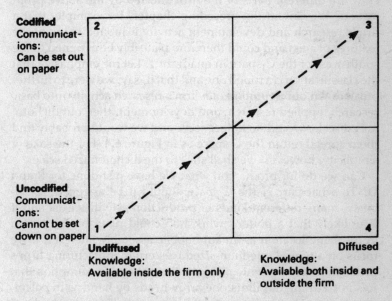

Figure 6.3 *Dichotomized scales for enterprise analysis.*

A more vivid way of restating the proposition would be to say that it is easier to get certain types of data by digging in the files than by opening up someone's cranium and rummaging around. Of course, the non trivial implication of this point is that, if you do not wish to share the information contained in your files with other employees or with the tea lady, then you had better lock up your files. In other words, the more formalized transactional knowledge becomes, the greater the need to set up barriers to its diffusion in order to make sure that it does not end up in undesirable places. These barriers are never foolproof. Witness the endless 'leaks' to the press of confidential cabinet papers that are presumably entombed in stainless steel vaults. Controlling the diffusion of information can be a costly and uncertain business.

Enterprise Subcultures in the C-Space

How are different parts of the firm affected by the above proposition? We saw in the preceding chapter, for example, that a firm's research and development activity exhibited many of the features of a fief and could therefore plausibly be assigned to the south-west of the C-space in quadrant 1. Let me emphasize that the classification is a rough one and that if, say, we were to further break down our definition of a firm's research activity into basic research, applied research, and development, then our dichotomized scales would no longer serve and we would probably find them spread out in the C-space as in Figure 6.4. For the sake of simplicity, however, we shall stick to the dichotomized scale.

Can we do for production what we have just done for R and D? To what part of the C-space should it be assigned? Obviously, many different kinds of production activities exist and it is unlikely that a potter's workshop could plausibly be placed in the same location as an automobile assembly line. Yet, if we focus on a typical, medium-sized western manufacturing firm's production department and make the unheroic assumption that it is not turning out flintstone arrowheads by hand as in paleolithic times, what might we see? First, we shall see standardized production procedures, a copious use of parts drawings, production schedules, and so on. Second, we shall see people on the shop floor whose observable behaviour is extensively constrained by the information contained in these documents. A

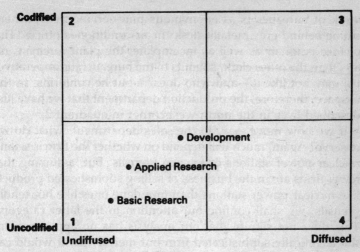

Figure 6.4 *R and D in the C-Space.*

lathe operator sets up a piece to be worked in a particular way, stands in a given place while operating the machine, carries out a predictable sequence of movements, does not leave his workstation without reason, and so on. Finally, we may notice that different people work to different documents. The information needed by the lathe operator may specify the number of units to be produced to a given design, their tolerance and critical dimensions. The scheduler will want more aggregated information on production plans, load factors, machine maintenance schedules, and labour rates. The flow of production information in the workshop – who gets what information, when, and what for – is fully specified in advance. If the diffusion of data to different people in the plant were not carefully regulated, chaos would quickly follow. Thus, in this simple example, production is characterized by an extensive use of codified information whose diffusion is carefully controlled. Tasks, and the relationship between tasks, are fully specified, payments and bonuses are directly related to the effective performance of these tasks, and task information only flows along the prescribed channels. We are in the world of bureaucracy, of the rational, standardized and controlled transaction. We tend to think of bureaucrats as anonymous time-serving pen pushers sitting behind grey metallic desks in air-conditioned offices. The picture is unfair as well as incomplete; the plant foreman, no less than the office clerk, submits to the bureaucratic imperative. He may not like it – and who does? – but he conforms. In the C-space, therefore, the production department that we have just described lives in the north-west corner in quadrant 2.

If we now move, say, to the sales department, what do we observe? Again, much will depend on whether the firm is selling nuclear power stations or kitchen utensils. But, assuming that fewer firms are in the business of selling sophisticated products like nuclear power stations than mundane ones like household utensils, we shall confine our attention to the latter category. This does not signify that our analysis has no application for the technically sophisticated firm but merely that it would call for some adaptation for which we have no space.

Interesting differences with the production department immediately appear. For a start, the majority of salesmen are nowhere to be seen. They are out and about selling to customers all over the country and perhaps even abroad. How do we know this since we cannot actually see them? Well, to be honest, we do not know for sure that half of them are not indeed lying in bed with a hangover. In fact, they do not work *in* the sales department in any physical sense, they *report* to it. But since the sales department manager is not in the habit of sending people around to check up on who is still lying in bed at ten o'clock, how on earth does he control his salesmen's activities? Simply by putting them on commission. Salesmen compete with each other for end of month bonuses and work in most cases independently of each other and largely outside the firm. Much of the information that they depend on for their effectiveness is well codified and generally available: the price of competing products, their performance and technical specifications, customer lists, and so on.

Salesmen are hard to control by bureaucratic methods. Staff turnover is high and many organizations employ either a part-time or an outside salesforce. A salesman's achievement does not consist in obeying detailed instructions to the letter as does a lathe operator's. It consists in going down into the marketplace and fighting for customers and market share. The salesman is *par excellence* a creature of the market quadrant so that the information environment of the sales department would place it in the north-east region of the C-space in quadrant 3.

As a final example of organizational transaction in the C-space, let us take the boardroom. Sitting as it does at the very top of the organizational pyramid, being the recipient of information flowing up the hierarchy and ultimately controlling what flows down, it might be tempting to place the board in the bureaucratic quadrant. As we shall show, this would be a mistake.

Take, for instance, the case of upward flowing information. Clearly, not *all* information flows up to the board. It does not, for example, decide on how many pencils will be bought in January for the typing pool of the customer service department. Nor does it pronounce on whether Mrs Whimper of the buying department will be allowed to take an extra five days' holiday in February this year so that she can visit a sister in Canada who has just given birth to twins. If the board were habitually immersed in such trivia it would quickly become a target for a weekly comedy series on television. No. The board makes the big uncertain decisions that no one else can make. What flows up the hierarchy is information concerning issues which cannot be solved at the lower level. Management by exception, in effect, pushes non-routine uncodified knowledge towards the top of the pyramid, leaving the base to deal with the more codified residue of routines and standard operating procedures. But such uncodified information can only really be dealt with through face-to-face procedures. Decisions at board level require extensive discussion, negotiation and, ultimately, consensus. A set of shared values, then, becomes an important requirement for a board to function effectively.

Given the uncodified nature of board transactions, does not its hierarchical position at the top of the pyramid place it in the fief quadrant? The answer must be: yes, if one is looking at its relationship with the next level of the organization's pyramid. But if one is concentrating, as we are here, on its internal structure, then it is a fief only in pathological cases; only when board members are under the spell of a strong charismatic and/or authoritarian chairman whose decisions they are merely called upon to rubber stamp.

In the more typical case, the board functions like a clan, mediating the relationship between the firm and the external environment. It has a scanning function, if you will, picking up ambiguous external signals from the wider environment and matching them with ambiguous internal signals on the firm's ability to respond. Most of the information it deals with is more often than not generally available to people outside the firm – the shape of the economy, political developments, technical breakthroughs – but much of it is uncodified, and reasonable men may disagree as to how to integrate into coherent patterns and then interpret the wide variety of data with which the board is bombarded. The board, then, is governed by a number of informal 'club rules' that reflect the shared values through which members relate to each other and go about their business. The board belongs to quadrant 4 of the C-space.

Management Styles

The information environment required by the three organizational units that we have just discussed, together with the R and D department dealt with in the last chapter, suggests their assignment in the C-space like that shown in Figure 6.5. A more discriminating set of scales would in theory allow all departments of a firm to find a home in the space.

Figure 6.5 is not just a pretty picture. It tells us something about the management style that we might expect to find in different parts of a firm. For example, if we hold that a research department is a fief, then we should expect informal authority relations to count for more than they do in the boardroom – a clan. Again, formal authority relations would be expected to be more important to the proper functioning of a production department than of a sales department in which detailed control is difficult to establish. By contrast, we would expect the typical transaction of the production and sales departments taken

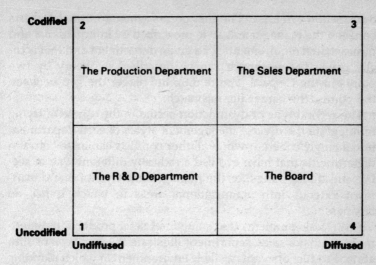

Figure 6.5 *Organizational Units in the C-Space.*

together to be much less personalized than those that characterize the boardroom or the R and D department. Ambiguous data is best transmitted in face-to-face relationships that require time to build up and perhaps call for a certain amount of interpersonal trust.

We have in this diagram, then, a testable set of simple propositions concerning management style. Crudely stated, they are the following:

1 Effective R and D departments are managed like fiefs

2 Effective Production departments are managed like bureaucracies

3 Effective Sales departments are managed like markets

4 Effective Boards are managed like clans

These propositions would need a great deal of elaboration and refinement before yielding useful results but, if corroborated, they would convert the C-space into a useful diagnostic tool for looking at dysfunctional management styles. Two types of dysfunction can arise. The first occurs when a mismatch exists between the management style prescribed by informational and transactional requirements for a given department and that actually used. The mismatch can be described in theory by two points in the C-space (Figure 6.6); the bigger the gap between the points, the bigger the mismatch.

The second type of dysfunction occurs in the course of trying to integrate the diverse management styles of each department into a single coherent whole. Either conflicts can arise between departments that have evolved a radically different way of seeing and doing things, or the management style of one department extends into organizational areas in which it has no business.

The classic problems that sometimes set a production department against a sales department illustrate the first type of situation. Production wants a stable environment in which planning and scheduling can take place and bureaucratic control can be exercised with a minimum amount of disturbance. Sales, by contrast, wants responsiveness to unforeseen threats and opportunities: a large order on a short deadline, a competitor's improved delivery schedule, and so on. If the sales department has its way, it injects unwanted turbulence into the production department's environment. If the production department predominates, the sales department can no longer respond in a timely way to external threats and opportunities. Something has to give. And, more often than not, it is the goodwill that keeps the two departments working together.

The second situation – departmental hegemony – sometimes follows upon the first. Suppose, for example, that production gets its way in this tug o'war between the two departments. It simply hands over to sales delivery schedules for different categories of goods together with standard product specifications. The sales department, constrained by production's behaviour, can no longer respond to customer requests adaptively and is reduced to merely allocating output. In fact, its style is 'bureaucratized' by the production department. It becomes 'production oriented' rather than 'marketing oriented'. If, however, the lines of influence ran in the other direction, from sales

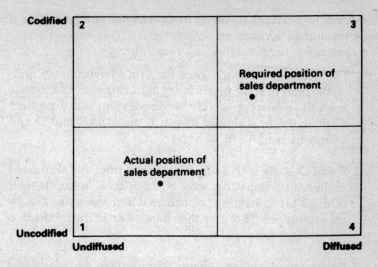

Figure 6.6 *Organizational Mismatch in the C-Space.*

to production, so that the latter ended up being more marketing oriented, the result would not necessarily be detrimental. Only a careful analysis of a department's real transactional requirements can tell us where it should be located in the C-space. Figure 6.5 can, at present, only serve as a rough guide and should therefore be used with care. There may be many valid reasons why some R and D departments should be run as clans and some sales departments should adopt a bureaucratic style. What C-D theory offers is an analytical tool with the help of which the argument for and against a particular assignment in the C-space may be made.

Integrating Subcultures through the Knowledge Cycle

The need to integrate the work of a variety of departments, each working with distinctive management styles, goes well beyond the necessity of preserving harmonious working relations. It turns out that the knowledge cycle discussed in Chapter Four endows the process of integration with a logic of its own, and particularly in the case of the innovative firm. Consider the

125

sequence of activities involved in developing and launching a new product or service:

1 The board of directors scans the firm's environment and, on the basis of some pretty fuzzy data, carries out a strategic analysis following which it decides in what product markets the firm should invest. It instructs R and D and orients its work in those areas.

2 R and D starts with a vaguely defined brief and through a sequence of steps that may go from basic research right through to engineering crystallizes it into one or more product prototypes. These are then handed on to the production department for a trial run.

3 Production develops a manufacturing plan and starts trial production. As it does so, it begins to standardize both the production process and certain product features. At a certain point it is ready for the product launch and the new product is then handed on to sales.

4 Sales tests out the new product in the market and, together with the customer, undergoes a learning process. Through trial and error the product is modified and improved, and the experience accumulating in the market place is then used by the firm's board of directors to further refine and develop the organization's product market strategy.

The highly schematic description of the steps through which a firm innovates corresponds to those of the knowledge cycle, namely, scanning, problem solving, diffusion and absorption (Figure 6.7). The departments assigned to different points in the C-space now turn out to be the relay stations that keep the cycle activated. We have in effect described a large feedback loop through which a firm absorbs stimuli from its environment and then responds but, unlike the more simple Stimulus-Response models of early behaviourist theories, a thinking process – i.e.

through codification and absorption – intervenes to rob the feed-back loop of any deterministic flavour (Figure 6.8).

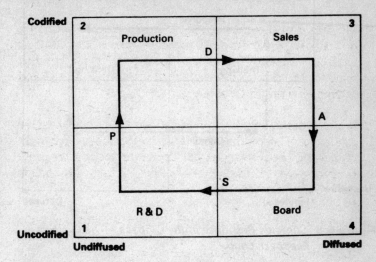

Figure 6.7 *Organizational Innovation in the C-Space.*

The knowledge cycle, then, finds one of its real world counter-parts in the organizational processes through which a firm inno-vates. This has important implications:

- The knowledge cycle measures a firm's ability to respond to its external environment: what kind of signals will it pick up? how will it interpret them? how will it respond and how fast?

- The positioning of departments in the C-space affects the size and shape of the cycle (refer back to Figure 4.4, p. 91). Different cycle configurations express different capacities to innovate. Dysfunctional positions do not just affect a given department. They affect the organizations's capacity as a whole.

- Failure to integrate the work of different departmental management styles leads to deformations or blockages in the cycle and a consequent loss of performance.

127

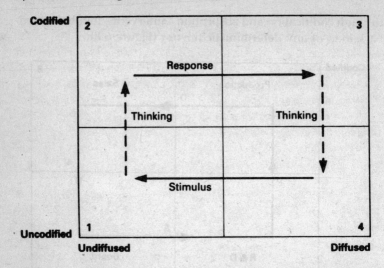

Figure 6.8 *Stimulus-Response in the C-Space – The Cycle as a Feedback Loop.*

- Managing the cycle as a whole is the responsibility of top management. It is from the successful management of the knowledge cycle that a distinctive *corporate* culture emerges. The trick is to strike a balance between the integrative needs of a corporate management style – the need to manage the cycle as a whole – and the need to manage its constituent elements.

A further implication that will be explored in more detail in the next two chapters concerns organizational growth. Where an organization's future development is indissolubly tied to the evolution of a technical or product innovation, it will have to follow the knowledge cycle and adapt its transactional style accordingly. This is basic to the problems of organizational change. The organization must invest in the creation of organizational units in the C-space that allow it to follow the cycle. Thus the Californian research-based start-up must develop production capacities, the production driven organization must invest in marketing and distribution – the number one problem today of state-owned enterprises in socialist and formerly socialist economies – and so on. But each organizational investment imposes a constraint on the firm's transactional style and makes any subsequent investments that might be designed to change the style that much more difficult. What starts out as a fief, with growth, sooner or later must accommodate a bureaucracy and then later on a market. As we shall see, not all firms can do this. Indeed, not all firms need to.

Industry Evolution in the C-Space

Finally, when an innovation or new technology is pervasive and spills out beyond the boundaries of one firm, when a whole group of firms face the problems of metamorphosing from fiefs to bureaucracies and then to markets, more or less at the same time, in order to follow the knowledge cycle, then we may speak of *industry evolution*, a phenomenon in which four phases can be distinguished:

1 **A Start-up Phase**
   Small research intensive entrepreneurial firms develop and launch a new technology around which a future industry will grow. These firms operate a highly personalized management style that usually revolves around their founder or their owner. They are typically fiefs.

2 **A Monopolistic Phase**
   Certain firms grow to a large size based upon a combination of market growth and the possession of proprietary knowledge. The critical asset in this phase is production capacity. The management style of such firms now becomes impersonal and formalized and their monopolistic positions allow them to behave as *bureaucracies*.

3 **A Competitive Phase**
   Demand stops growing and firms start to compete with each other on the basis of price and the ability to distribute rapidly and responsively. To compete effectively in this way, firms need to acquire a *market* culture.

129

4 An Oligopolistic Phase

Survivors of the shakeout that occurred in the competitive phases move towards non price forms of competition such as product differentiation, advertising and services. In this phase, firms can only avoid cut-throat competition and adjust to each other's presence in the market if they behave like *clans*.

Industry evolution can also be described in the C-space (Figure 6.9). Tying the industrial life cycle concept in this way to the knowledge cycle tells us a great deal about the emergence and decline of various types of industrial culture and their preferred transactional styles. As the diagram implies, industry evolution is in large part technology driven.

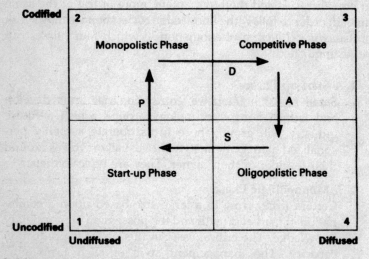

Figure 6.9 *The Cyclical Evolution of Industry in the C-Space.*

Conclusion

What we have done in this chapter is to take a general theory concerning the cultural use of information and apply it to a specific institutional entity: the industrial firm. We have matched transactional patterns with organizational units and shown how the cyclical flow of new knowledge over time, embodied in technology and procedures, poses both problems of cultural and organizational adjustment. In effect a triangular relationship links technology, organizational culture, and organizational structure (Figure 6.10).

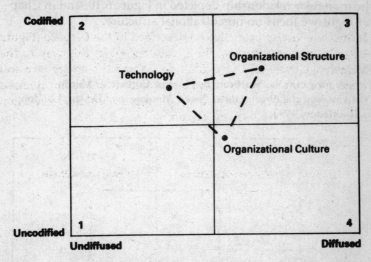

Figure 6.10 *Positioning the Firm's Technology, Structure, and Culture in the C-Space.*

Organizational specialists usually have few problems in seeing a link between technology and organizational structure;[1] a large automated manufacturing system, for instance, tends to require a deep pyramid of planning and control systems; a small potter's shop, conversely, requires only a small flat pyramid. But many of these specialists have had problems with culture and have resorted to treating it as a kind of residual phenomenon injected into the system to give it some 'oomph'. By contrast, we have made culture – information structuring and sharing – central to our analysis.

Technology, organization, and culture are complementary inputs into a firm's operations. There must be a fit between them in the C-space. The movement of knowledge in the space is constantly pulling and pushing them around so that a fit is never final or stable and must constantly be resought. The C-space allows us to study the fit, or lack of it, between the three variables and to develop a unified view of the problem of organization, cultural and technical change.

In the next chapter we focus on the technological vertex of the triangular relationship depicted in Figure 6.10, and in Chapter Eight we focus on organizational structure.

Reference
1. See, for example, Scarbrough, H., and Corbett, J. Martin, *Technology and Organization: Power, Meaning, and Design*, London: Routledge, 1992.

7

Technology

Introduction

According to cultural anthropologists, technology is the dynamic expression of culture, an embodiment of knowledge, values, and beliefs in useful artefacts and in the activities, individual or social, that we associate with their use. In the last chapter we saw that knowledge could be embodied in objects, in documents, or in the heads of people. Technology, then, is to do with the way these different forms of knowledge come together to deliver something useful, combining in ways that are often constrained by prevailing beliefs and values. In many countries, for example, superstition disallows a thirteenth floor on buildings, and in the former Soviet Union the possession of a typewriter was controlled by a licensing system.

In the sense that we shall be using it, therefore, technology is very broad, being essentially concerned with the way that knowledge is *patterned* across the objects, documents, and heads in which it is stored, and also with the way it is subsequently activated. In effect, we can think of technology as sets of data, however stored, that are brought into some kind of systematic relationship with each other as indicated in Figure 7.1.

To the extent that these relationships are 'wired in' we can think of technology as hardware. Most mechanical contraptions have this characteristic. The mechanical motion of a pedal on a bicycle, for example, translates directly into the mechanical motion of a wheel. Yet in many technological devices these relationships are not fixed and can be activated in various ways. Where the inputs required to activate them, although variable, are themselves well defined, we can think of technology as software: for example the different functions on the keyboard

133

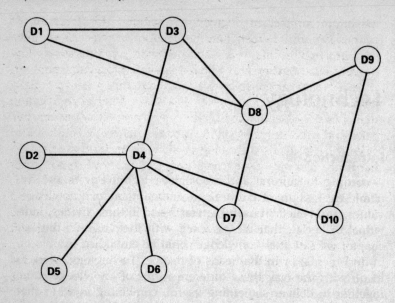

Figure 7.1 *Technology as Interrelated Data Sets.*

of my PC, although well defined, can be activated in any sequence that I choose providing that certain conventions are respected. Where the inputs are fuzzy, however, so that even their definition requires a certain amount of deliberation, then we begin to think of technology as a human skill, whether expressed through individual or through organizational processes. Deciding at what levels to set the variables of a corporate financial simulation may require considerable technical experience and know-how and may be subject to discussion and debate among a group of experts.

We can thus position a firm's technologies along a hard-soft continuum at one end of which we find hardware with at most one degree of freedom – a spanner or a screwdriver, for example, will only allow one kind of movement when used as intended; at the other end we find what some have called 'orgware': clusters of technologies that are organized to offer a maximum number of degrees of freedom. This freedom, of course, is nothing other than the freedom to code. As we have seen in Chapter One, it is associated with a comparatively low degree of codification and a high degree of information content.

As a general proposition we might say that organizationally embodied technologies operate at a lower level of codification than physically embodied technologies even if administrative rules and procedures try to increase the degree of codification.

Viewing a firm's technologies as something more than its hardware has recently become very popular and considerably extends the scope of its strategic options. Gary Hamel and C. K. Prahalad talk about core competencies, and Stalk, Evans and Shulman refer to organizational capabilities.[1] These can be thought of as two different levels of incorporation of the soft organizational element in the definition of technology.

In Figure 7.2, for example, we depict three different levels at which a technology can be represented. In the diagram the smallest nodes are all hardware with, typically, relatively few degrees of freedom. The intermediate nodes cluster these hardware elements together and interlink them. Some of these links will be 'hard' and fixed and amenable to automation; they also enjoy few degrees of freedom. They are depicted by thick solid lines. Other links, by contrast, already incorporate a considerable amount of soft know-how, whether embodied in documents or in implicit organizational practices. These links are depicted by thinner, dotted lines. These intermediate nodes are what Hamel and Prahalad would refer to as core competencies. The outer circle now clusters core competencies into organization-wide capabilities. It is the softest level at which a firm's technology can be represented. Since competencies already enjoy more degrees of freedom than most 'hard' technologies, coupling them together in this way multiplies the degrees of freedom that inhere in organizational technologies even more.

Technology as a Portfolio, Technology as a System

Many firms like to view their technologies as a portfolio of assets. This seems a natural thing to do. Certain items in

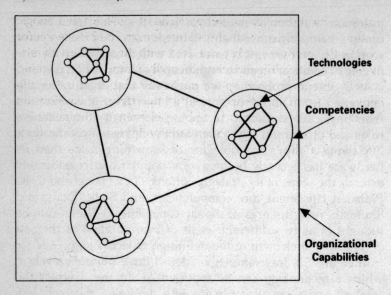

Figure 7.2 *Levels of Representation of Technology.*

the portfolio will have been there longer than others. New technologies have to be brought into the portfolio, whether through external acquisition or through internal development; older technologies must be phased out of the portfolio. Thus a portfolio can be balanced in terms of risks and uncertainty, resources allocated, returns expected, etc.

Yet portfolio reasoning applied to technology is but an extension of portfolio reasoning applied to product-markets, a practice that was popularized by the Boston Consulting Group in the late 1960s and still widely applied today. We must ask how justified is its extension to thinking about technology.

There have been several portfolio techniques developed since BCG's. Most of them seek to relate the attractiveness of opportunities in a given product-market – whether measured by market share, life cycle, or by some other indicators – to a firm's competitive position within that product-market. Figure 7.3 illustrates a typical product-market portfolio. It indicates two things: firstly where the firm actually stands – each bubble stands for a particular product-market and its size might represent its relative importance to the firm; and secondly where the firm would actually like to be – i.e. in the northwest corner. It is the gap between current and desired position that triggers decisions on whether to invest in moving a given element in the portfolio, in removing it from the portfolio, or in bringing in new elements into the portfolio.

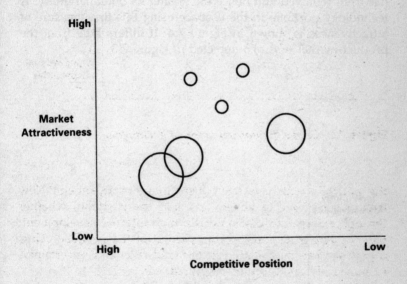

Figure 7.3 *A Product-Market Portfolio.*

Would a portfolio of technologies lend itself to the same kinds of decisions as a portfolio of products in their respective markets? And could the C-space be used for this purpose? The answer to both questions is a qualified yes.

Technologies, like product-markets, can be analysed in terms of their attractiveness and the competitiveness that they offer a firm. In the C-space, a technology's competitive position can be assessed from its position along the diffusion axis: what percentage of competitors possess the relevant codified and uncodified knowledge required to operate the technology? In this respect, the further to the left one can locate a firm's technology, the more competitive it will turn out to be.

Attractiveness might be measured in two ways that are complementary. The first positions a technology along the codification scale as a function of how far it has been developed, debugged, and standardized. The higher up the codification scale a technology can be located, the more technical uncertainty has been removed and hence the greater its potential utility. A technology portfolio in the C-space using this first measure of attractiveness is shown in Figure 7.4. It differs little from the product-market portfolio depicted in Figure 7.3.

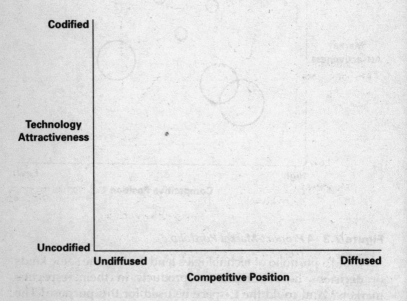

Figure 7.4 *A Technology Portfolio.*

Recall from Figure 7.2, however, that a technology can be represented as a series of interlinked nodes, that is to say, as a *system* (see Figure 7.5). This suggests that in certain situations – for example, when the links are strong – acting on one node will have an effect on other nodes. To illustrate: If Nissan were ever to succeed in reducing a real car engine to the size of a pinhead, it would radically modify every other element of car design. Thus, in contrast to a product-market portfolio in which the different elements can be handled discretely – get into this market here, get out of that product line there, etc. – a technology portfolio requires that the degree of interconnection of its constituent elements be taken into account first.

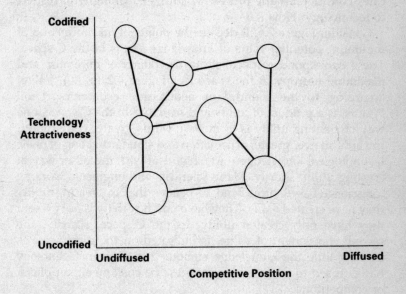

Figure 7.5. *Technology as a System.*

Here is where a second measure of attractiveness suggests itself when making technological choices: how far do the benefits yielded by investing in a given node propagate to the rest of the technological system through the links that bind it together? The answer, of course, will depend on the degree of interconnectedness that exists between the different elements that make up a technology portfolio. Some technologies and competencies will be very tightly coupled together, others much less so. Only in the latter case can technologies be dealt with discretely without losing some important benefits.

The Paradox of Value

A C-space based representation of a technology portfolio also differs from product-market portfolios in another important way: Knowledge assets move around the C-space according to the precepts of codification-diffusion theory and this complicates considerably the process of strategy-making with respect to technology. How so?

Consider Figure 7.6. It depicts the points of maximum and of minimum potential value of knowledge assets in the C-space. These correspond respectively to the points of minimum and maximum entropy in the space (see Figure 4.2, p. 80). Value, according to the founder of neoclassical economics, Leon Walras, is a product of utility and scarcity.[2] In the C-space, one way of creating utility is to move towards greater codification, towards an ever greater articulation and standardization of one's technological knowledge – we shall deal with the other way of creating utility shortly. Many scientists and engineers working for science-based firms tend to believe that in creating utility they have created value. They have not. If scarcity is not present they have only created utility. In the C-space, scarcity, the second component of value, is indicated on the diffusion axis by how little the knowledge embodied in a given technology has diffused to others, whether these be customers, suppliers, or competitors.

The equation that we are establishing between maximum value and minimum entropy suggests that value can be considered the economic equivalent of appropriable energy, that is, energy available to do work for an individual or a firm, or what economists call an *economic rent*. The second law of thermodynamics, however, tells us that in a closed system, entropy can only increase. In the language of the C-space, this tells us that, left to their own devices, economic values or rents can only

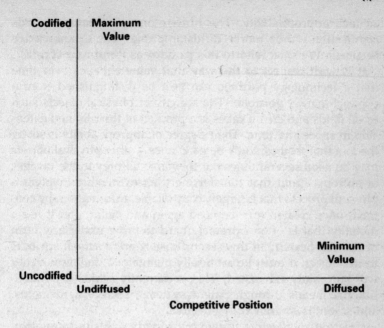

Figure 7.6 *The Value of Knowledge Assets in the C-Space.*

erode. As Georgescu-Roegen puts it in his book *The Entropy Law and the Economic Process*, 'from the purely physical viewpoint, the economic process is entropic: it neither creates nor consumes matter or energy, but only transforms low into high entropy'.[3] The end point of this erosion process in an economic system, of course, is market equilibrium, just as in physical systems it is thermal equilibrium.

Maximizing the value of one's technological assets in the C-space means locating them as close as possible to the north-west corner of the space where maximum value obtains. *But we know from C-D theory that this is the least stable region in the space since, given its high degree of codification, it is the region from which knowledge is most likely to diffuse rapidly.* Creating value through technological assets thus confronts the paradox that the closer one gets to creating utility the more difficult it becomes to achieve appropriability. The further one progresses towards codification, the more diffusion-prone one's knowledge becomes. We shall refer to this paradox as *the paradox of value*.

It is with respect to the way that value behaves over time that a technology portfolio can best be distinguished from a product-market portfolio. The scarcity of physical objects such as oil fields and cream cakes is a product of their limited extension in space and time. Their degree of appropriability is set by the fact that they can only be used once – other physical objects may be used several times but they are still prey to the ravages of entropy – and that transferring their ownership involves a physical process that is largely controllable. Information, by contrast, once created, can be used again and again, and it has a mobility that is often extremely hard to bring under any form of control. Scarcity in this second case is not a *natural* attribute to the object; it must be artificially maintained, failing which it will be rapidly exhausted. This is currently achieved by institutional means through patent systems, secrecy agreements, and so on; it is rarely fully effective.

Creating an effective system of property rights in technological and other forms of knowledge will be one of the great challenges of the emerging information society. To judge by the difficulties that many firms encounter in preventing pirating and imitation of their designs and ideas, progress is likely to be very slow. What options are available in the meantime to firms that confront the paradox of value?

Two Responses to the Paradox

Firms can deal with the paradox of value in two quite distinct ways, each of which reflects the nature of the technologies they possess as well as the competitive dynamics of the industry they operate in. The technologies a firm possesses establish its basic technological endowment, whereas the relevant industry dynamics specifies the environment in which that endowment has to be used. In some cases a mix of the two approaches will be called for, something that requires a particularly clear grasp of what is at issue.

Drawing on military jargon we might label our first option a *war of position* and our second option a *war of movement*.

A war of position is pursued in the belief that a firm's best option for extracting value from its technology portfolio is to accumulate as many relevant technologies as possible – these are treated as discrete entities – in the northwest corner of the C-space and to keep them there as long as it can. It is recognized that sooner or later these technologies will diffuse towards the right in the space and the idea is to make sure that it will be later rather than sooner. In effect, a war of position aims to bring the knowledge cycle to a halt in the northwest corner of the C-space and, through the creation of barriers to diffusion such as patents, secrecy agreements, or economies of scale, to prevent technological rents from being eroded by competitive forces. According to this perspective, once a technology reaches the market region of the C-space and is available to all at a competitive price, it has little strategic interest for the firm.

A war of position can be schematically represented as in Figure 7.7. The diagram locates three distinct types of technology in the C-space:

- Base technologies are those that, being well codified and well diffused, constitute the common possession of an industry. In themselves they offer a firm little or no competitive advantage, but without them a firm is not even considered an industry player. Just-in-Time manufacturing in the car industry, for example, has become a base technology.

- Emergent technologies are neither well codified nor diffused outside a firm. They are still coming out of its research laboratories. Although they are considered to be potentially valuable for a firm, no one is in a position to firmly predict their prospects. High temperature superconductivity would today be considered an emergent technology.

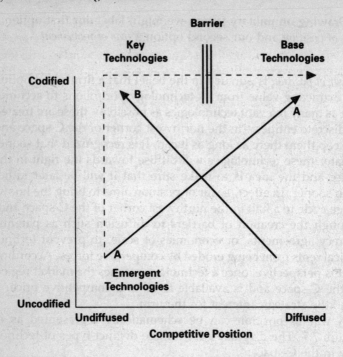

Figure 7.7 *Base, Emergent and Key Technologies in the C-Space.*

- Key technologies have been codified but have not yet diffused outside the firm. Where they allow a firm to distinguish its offering from those of its competitors they constitute an important competitive advantage and become a source of economic rent. For many years, float glass manufacturing processes were considered a key technology for Pilkington's.

Figure 7.7 indicates that, unless otherwise constrained, the natural trajectory for an emergent technology is to follow the diffusion curve A A' and to gradually diffuse as they become more standardized and codified. At A' an emergent technology has become a base technology available to all and incapable by itself of yielding an economic rent. Only if a technology's trajectory can somehow be diverted towards the northwest corner of the C-space – that is to say, if some way can be found to counter the natural forces of diffusion – can an emergent technology be converted into a key technology. For this to happen, somewhere along the curve A A', a technology would have to be hijacked by the arrow B, dragged into the northwest corner, and kept there. It is a risky and costly operation that can only be financially justified if a technology, once brought into the northwest corner, can be held captive there for a reasonable length of time. On one interpretation, part of Britain's economic failure can be put down to its unwillingness or inability to perform such a hijacking operation. The country has proved to be an excellent source of emergent technologies – the jet engine, the computer, penicillin, etc. – which its firms have consistently failed to convert into key technologies.

A war of movement adopts quite a different approach. It is predicated on the assumption that sometimes a firm has more to gain from running with – and possibly faster than – the knowledge cycle than from trying to stop it. A war of movement, no less than a war of position, seeks to extract value from knowledge assets in the northwest corner of the C-space and thus to make it part of a technology's itinerary as it progresses through the space. The key difference between the two approaches, however, is that whereas the second tries to block the erosion of a firm's technological assets for as long as possible by setting up hefty barriers to its diffusion, the first is not only prepared to release many of its key technologies, but *actively to promote their diffusion*. Why is this so?

The main reason is that whereas in a war of position one treats technology as a *stock*, in a war of movement one treats it as a *flow*. In the first approach the aim is to maximize the *quantity* of technology that accumulates in the northwest corner of the C-space; in the second, one is concerned to maximize the *throughput* of technology in that region. *Each entails a different way of conceiving a firm's technological assets*. As was mentioned above, a war of position requires that a firm's technological assets be treated as discrete entities; a war of movement, by contrast, views these assets as *an integrated and highly interconnected system* in which value can propagate from one part of the system to another through its constituent links.

Where technologies are discrete their value is intrinsic. When they are released, their value goes with them. Where technologies are interconnected, however, part of their value may be intrinsic, but part of it also resides in the links they have established between themselves. When such technologies are selectively released some of their value may go with them, but much of it will stay behind in the links that still bind them to technologies that the firm continues to retain, *and this latter type of value may actually be enhanced if the effect of releasing one technology is to increase the demand for and hence the relative scarcity of the technologies that remain in the firm's possession*.

The difference between treating technology as stock and treating it as flow is illustrated in Figure 7.8. It is clear that in the first case maximizing value entails damming up the knowledge cycle in order to accumulate technology assets behind diffusion barriers, whereas in the second case it involves exploiting the cycle in order to maximize the throughput in the northwest corner of the C-space.

How does one choose which type of 'war' to conduct?

In effect the choice is conditioned by the two variables we have been discussing: the characteristics of the firm's technologies themselves and the competitive dynamics of the industry or industries that the firm operates in.

Technologies

A firm's technologies may be more or less interconnected and hence more or less amenable to being handled like a system. A firm like Boeing, for example, operates a far more integrated set of technologies than, say, a firm like Unilever. The former is thus more likely to deal with its technology assets as systems than the latter, which will tend to view them as discrete entities. Many technologies are something of a hybrid; for some purposes they can be thought of as inte-

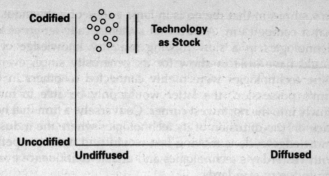

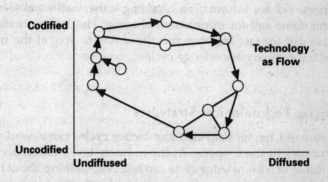

Figure 7.8 *Technology as Stock versus Technology as Flow.*

grated, for others they have to be considered discrete. Also technologies can evolve in either direction – i.e. towards systems or towards discreteness. A critical skill, therefore, involves recognizing what is happening to a technology or to an interconnected network of technologies over time.

Competitive Dynamics

In Chapter Six we tied an industry's life cycle to the knowledge cycle and the industry's evolution to both. It suggests that the rate at which knowledge can pass through the northwest corner of the C-space is only partially under the firm's control and that therefore the scope it has for maximizing throughput in that region is in large part set by the industry that it competes in. A firm that systematically let go of key technologies in a slow moving industry knowledge cycle would have little to show for its generosity since, even if these technologies were highly connected to others in the firm's possession, the latter would only be able to move slowly into the northwest corner. Conversely, a firm that held back on the diffusion of its technologies where the industry knowledge cycle is moving fast would find itself competing with yesterday's technologies and unable to influence evolving industry standards.

To summarize, we might say that some competitive situations call for information hoarding – the traditional view – and some call for information sharing. The latter situations also call for fast learning and the ability to stay at the front of the industry knowledge cycle.

Generic Technological Strategies

We saw in Chapter Four that knowledge cycles can have different shapes in the C-space. At the industry level, differences in the shape of a knowledge cycle can tell us something about how an industry or groups of firms within an industry compete.

Consider Figure 7.9. It depicts a deep knowledge cycle confined to the left of the space. Such a cycle will be found in many small to medium sized technology based firms, such as biotechnology companies or Silicon Valley start-ups. In cycle terms, the critical technological skills deployed by such firms are problem solving and absorption. Since many of these firms are either too small to afford hefty barriers to the diffusion of their codified technologies – patents, after all, cost money to protect – or operate in industries that are too fast moving to make it worth their while, effective absorption, the learning-by-doing through which they embed newly codified knowledge that they have created in a matrix of tacit know-how specific to the firms themselves, becomes critical to the maintenance of these firms' competitive advantage.

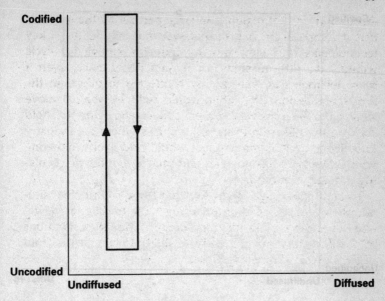

Figure 7.9 *A Deep Knowledge Cycle.*

Figure 7.10, by contrast, depicts a flat knowledge cycle located in the upper region of the space. We know from C-D theory that such a cycle, by dint of the high degree of codification of the knowledge it contains, will operate at much higher speeds than one located further down the space. Here the critical skills are scanning and diffusion, the ability to dialogue in a codified way with a large population in real time. It is characteristic of larger firms with strong capacities in market research and distribution, firms that are able to pick up market signals and respond to them before competitors do.

If small technology based start-ups lack the resources to distribute – i.e. diffuse – their new products on a large scale, large market-oriented firms tend to be uncomfortable operating at the degree of uncertainty and risk that these start-ups are willing to contemplate. In Figure 7.11 we combine their two cycles. What do we see? That they overlap in the maximum value region of the C-space. It is with respect to technological knowledge

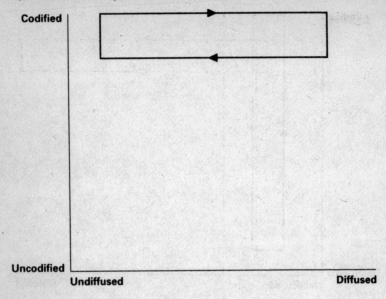

Figure 7.10 *A Flat Knowledge Cycle.*

that has reached this region that firms face a choice of *competing or collaborating*.

Thorn-EMI, for example, operating a deep cycle, developed a brilliant new technology, the CT-Scanner, but had neither the possibility of protecting it with a hefty barrier of patents nor the organizational skills to internalize the codified knowledge that it had created through absorption. It therefore arrived in the northwest corner of the C-space with few defences against predators. Once there, it encountered General Electric, operating a flat cycle with a large and well trained sales force, and a strong capacity to enhance the diffusion of the new technology by improving it incrementally in response to client expectations.

Unlike Thorn-EMI, Genetech, a biotechnology firm also operating a deep cycle, chose collaboration. Lacking the resources to invest in research and development at a rate which would allow it to maintain its lead in a deep knowledge cycle on the left of the C-space, it sold 60 per cent of its shares to

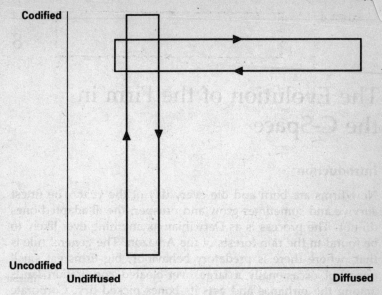

Figure 7.11 *Two Knowledge Cycles Combined.*

a much larger pharmaceutical firm with a strong distribution capability, Hoffman la Roche. In this second case, the two knowledge cycles operate synergistically. How synergistically is determined largely by how well two quite distinct corporate cultures fit together, the subject of Chapter Eleven.

References

1. Hamel, G., and Prahalad, C. K., 'The Core Competence of the Corporation', *Harvard Business Review*, May–June, 1990; Stalk, G., Evans, P., and Shulman, L. 'Competing on Capabilities: The New Rules of Corporate Strategy', *Harvard Business Review*, March–April, 1992.

2. Walras, L., *Elements of Pure Economics*, Philadelphia, PA: Orion Editions, 1984.

3. Georgescu-Roegen, N., *The Entropy Law and the Economic Process*, Cambridge, Mass: Harvard University Press, 1971.

8

The Evolution of the Firm in the C-Space

Introduction

New firms are born and die every day of the year. The fittest survive and sometimes grow and prosper, the ill-adapted ones do not. The process is as Darwinian as anything ever likely to be found in the rain forests of the Amazon. The general rule is that, where there is predatory behaviour, big firms eat small ones but occasionally a large over-bloated corporation lands among the pirhanas and gets its bones picked dry. Corporate demography deals with more variable life spans than are found in biological species – the House of Mitsui was already a formidable presence in eighteenth century Japan; and the French firm of Saint-Gobain is a creation of Colbert's – and some organizational forms appear to be more durable than others.

Survival is more than a matter of simply adapting to an external environment – after all, a corpse or a sand dune are perfect examples of adaptation *tout court* – the trick is to maintain the integrity and coherence of internal processes while doing so. In Chapter Six we gave such internal coherence a very particular meaning: the fit between a firm's technology, its organization and its culture. We also showed that this internal coherence is constantly threatened by the destabilizing action of knowledge flowing in and around the C-space. Some of this knowledge is the firm's own creation, but by far the largest part is imported from the external environment so that the evolution of a firm's technology and general know-how is inextricably linked to information flows outside the firm. A firm's organizational arrangements are thus facilitated or constrained by the wider institutional order, and a firm's management styles – its corporate and departmental cultures – draw heavily upon the cultural premises of the societies the firm operates in.

In this chapter, we shall look at organizational growth and development as a process of maintaining internal coherence in the face of external constraints. To do this involves using the C-space in a different way. In Chapter Six, where we dealt with problems of organizational differentiation and integration, the firm occupied the whole space, allowing us to spread departments as we wished anywhere within it. In this chapter we shall represent the culture of a firm, no matter what its size, by a single point in a C-space along whose diffusion axis is located the population of the firm's employees. A mechanical engineer would say that we are representing the firm through its cultural centre of gravity. In effect, we are working with its corporate culture rather than its diverse organizational sub-cultures. We are asking whether the management style of firm X, taken as a whole, is best described as a fief, a bureaucracy, a market, or a clan. Of course, some firms resist such a question and will resolutely occupy a central position in the C-space thus making them everything and nothing at the same time (Figure 8.1). The fact that some firms are not culturally distinctive is not necessarily a bad thing, however, and does not threaten the point we are trying to establish.

The chapter divides naturally into two parts. In the first, I shall briefly summarize some of the key features that first led to the growth of the large US corporation and then to the development of the multidivisional structure as a preferred way of organizing a diverse set of activities on a large scale. In the second part of the chapter, I shall try to interpret this evolution in the C-space in order to identify the role played by technological, organizational, and cultural adaptation when a firm responds and tries to adapt to external developments. Much of what follows in the first part draws upon the pioneering work of the Harvard business historian, Alfred Chandler.[1]

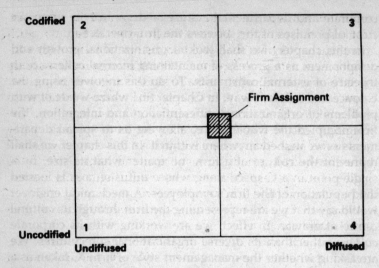

Figure 8.1 *The Culturally Non-distinctive Firm.*

Growing the Large Firm: The US Example

The industrial landscape of mid-nineteenth century America was populated by small single function family-owned firms that operated on a strictly regional basis. If you manufactured widgets in Vermont, then they were more likely to be sold in Vermont than elsewhere and there they would be sold by an independent distributor over whom you had little control. The situation could be schematized as in Figure 8.2 with goods and services flowing horizontally through the market from small firm to small firm until they reached the final consumer. Since the horse and the wagon were the dominant form of inland transportation, producers and consumers, by the very nature of things, could never be very distant from each other.

Then, in the 1880s, along came a technological revolution in

Figure 8.2 *Horizontal Market Transactions.*

154

communications in the shape of the railways and the telegraph. Not only did transport become much faster, it became much more reliable. A train timetable became one of technology's triumphs over nature. A locomotive could plough on at a steady speed across terrain inaccessible to horses, and neither rain nor snow could stop it. No more wheels stuck in three feet of slush and mud, or horses collapsing from cold and inanition. The telegraph also at this time replaced the pony express, a few taps of the finger achieving reliably in a few seconds what had hitherto required several weeks of sitting uncomfortably in the saddle. Thus mechanical motion was replacing animal motion, and electrical motion was replacing both.

What new vistas did these developments in technology open up for American firms?

The first was one of opportunities offered by the sudden integration of hitherto separate markets. Widgets sold in Vermont could now be sold in California, and those who responded to the new situation by expanding their market share would achieve important economies of scale that would further reinforce their competitive advantage. In a number of industries in which manufacturing economies of scale were potentially important, regional producers ceased to be competitive. There, the rapid expansion of the railways and the telegraph had transformed the United States into a single, integrated, national market that would only henceforth be accessible to those willing and able to invest in new manufacturing technologies, those that could exploit an expanded scale of operations.

The second vista opened up was towards the new administrative means available for seizing the newly expanded market opportunities. The capacity to communicate from coast to coast in seconds via the telegraph suddenly meant that it was cheaper to co-ordinate the flow of goods from production to markets using direct administrative controls within the firm itself than it was to rely on the indirect route of external agents acting in the market. The competitive firm in search of an increased share of a freshly created national market wanted its products to be stocked in the right quantities, at the right place, and at the right time. Passing through outside distributors, who most likely had other preoccupations to contend with, was unlikely to achieve the speed that telegraph-based administrative methods could now offer.

In sum, market integration offered a number of firms opportunities that could best be seized through a process of internal co-ordination in which hierarchy took the place of external markets as in Figure 8.3. The firms most favoured were those whose activities offered manufacturing, distribution, or administrative economies of scale and these often reinforced each other so that the standardization of a product allowed longer and more economic production runs – hence continuous production processes – easier distribution and hence lower administrative costs. If demand for the product were elastic, a virtuous circle was set in motion in which increased demand translated into

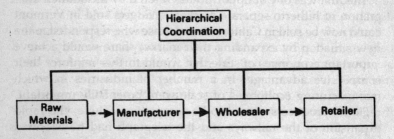

Figure 8.3 *Hierarchical Coordination.*

lower costs and lower costs once more into increased demand.

In this way, a number of firms grew large and national in scope while others, unable to break into this virtuous circle, remained steadfastly regional and hence comparatively small. The new giants were not just larger, they were in fact different kinds of animal from what had gone before. The new technologies that they were developing required considerably more skill and sophistication to operate – this was the age of the engineer, the man with a strong grounding in theory, and sense enough to know when to apply it. They also required investment on a large scale and hence a concern with financial efficiency and performance. So accountants, auditors, and financial personnel were also needed. In this period, too, the first professional managers made their appearance, people with the necessary skills in planning, co-ordination, and control, to keep track of thousands of transactions, simultaneously conducted throughout the national territory, and to weave them into a coherent and profitable corporate undertaking. More often than not, the skills required for managing on this scale put them beyond the reach of the traditional owner-manager. The new dispensation called for a separation of ownership and control. Trying to keep control of the running of the business in the family, even if an owner-manager had himself had the required competence, called for too many assumptions concerning the genius and the motivation of his progenies. If Junior wanted to become a beachcomber or a preacher, it was now wiser to let him go. The personalized, idiosyncratic, sometimes authoritarian, style of the owner-manager thus gradually gave way in a number of key sectors to the cool, detached, calculative approach of the professional manager.

Standardized operating procedures, impersonally and impartially applied, subjected to continued analytical scrutiny and improvement, exemplified the new approach: management by rule rather than management by fiat. The metamorphosis was extraordinary. In the 1870s, a large firm employed 10,000 people. By 1900, it was employing 100,000.

The sudden extension in organizational capacity was exploited by many firms who used it to extend their product lines and move into new areas. A captive distribution network could be used to sell ballbearings as well as widgets. And why not toy dolls and chewing gum? In the early decades of this century, to their cost, a number of large firms soon found out why. With an increase in the size and diversity of the firm's product lines, co-ordination costs started going up once more and a loss of specialization ensued. Widgets and chewing gum did not mix. One sold them to different people and in different ways. Hopefully, widgets had a longer shelf life than chewing gum and hopefully, too, chewing gum did not require any after sales services. If it did, it would be performed by dentists working independently of the firm. The functional structure of the large new enterprises was ill-adapted to cope with such diversity. What to do?

One possible answer to co-ordination problems is to decentralize and let horizontal co-ordination once more replace vertical co-ordination. But then, why not let the market do the job as it had done previously? There is certainly some force in the argument that claims that such firms had reached the natural limits of the size at which internal hierarchical co-ordination is competitive with external co-ordination through markets. Yet none of these firms returned to external markets to solve their problems. Instead, they changed the basic structure of their organizations. The outcome was the multi-divisional structure.[2]

The Switch to the Multidivisional Structure

By shifting the focus of specialization from functions such as marketing, finance and production to product groups or divisions as they came to be called, the firm did not in fact abolish functional co-ordination. It merely confined its scope to a particular division (Figure 8.4). Naturally this entailed some duplication as each division would now have to develop its own marketing, production and financial capacities. But the autonomy with which each division could now function allowed it to maintain and further develop the specialized competence which was the source of its competitive strength in the market. In effect, the multi-divisional structure became a collection of functional structures standing side by side and linked by common ownership.

But, here again, it might well be asked, who needs common ownership? What organizational advantage is to be had by linking a widget division with a chewing gum division? If co-ordination of *functions* appears to offer some clear cut advantages, the case for co-ordinating *product* divisions seems to be much less obvious. Where was the payoff?

In practice, there were two. Where the firm's product divisions were as diverse as widgets and chewing gum, the link between them was a holding company. Managers in the holding company acted as hard-nosed investors who allocated financial resources to the high performers and thus forced the divisions

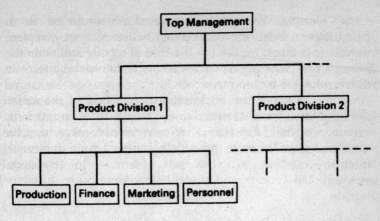

Figure 8.4 *The Functional Structure Subordinated to the Divisional Structure.*

to compete with each other for scarce investment resources. In such a case, the manager was merely acting as a substitute for the stock market. He was telling prospective investors in his firm that, both in his investment decisions and in the managerial performance that he could elicit from product divisions, he could outperform external capital markets. Internal capital markets worked with more copious information and greater skills in making use of it.

The investment logic of the divisional structure could be weakened or reinforced with an industrial logic that it also had to contend with. Reasoning in investment terms a manager would seek diversity in his divisional structure so as to create a portfolio balanced in terms of risks and returns. High risk, high return activities would co-exist with others, offering lower risks and lower returns. Average performance was what ultimately counted – the bottom line for the firm as a whole. Yet, the more diversified the divisional portfolio, the less credible became claims made on *managerial* grounds that the firm could outperform the market. Wherein lay its skill, in widgets or in chewing gum? Here, an industrial logic was asserting itself, a logic that seemed to be saying that high performance comes from sticking to one's knitting. Where divisions shared a common industrial or distribution base, the relationship between them was less intensively competitive than in the case of wholly autonomous divisions and was regulated by strategic considerations that were formulated by top management.

In sum, although the organizational structure of the large holding company and its subsidiaries – which, following current practice, we shall label *H-form* for convenience – was hard to distinguish from the more industrially cohesive multi-divisional structure – which we shall call *M-form* – in terms of organizational process and content they were quite different animals.

Interpreting Enterprise Evolution in the C-Space

Can the evolution of the large American firm that we have just traced out – European firms evolved in a similar fashion but with a lag of two or three decades – be represented in the C-space? And if so, what interpretation does it suggest?

The classic owner-managed family firm of mid-nineteenth century America typifies what we have called a fief. The management style was highly personalized and authoritarian: one man rule was the rule. A technological revolution in the means of communications that originated outside the firm changed all this. By suddenly placing within its geographical reach economic opportunities that had until then been quite inaccessible, the railroad and the telegraph triggered off a process of organizational development that led to a vast increase in the size of the firm that was in a position to respond. But at this new size the firm was no longer governable through the traditional network of personalized and informal authority relations. New procedures, more impersonal, and more systematic, were called for. Operating instructions, that could be given casually face to face when a subordinate occupied a desk in the next room, now had to be put down on paper when he was relocated to San Diego or to San Francisco.

In other words, a move up the C-space, towards greater codification and a more bureaucratic style of management, was the adaptive response to the technological stimulus just described. Since the growth in bureaucratic capacity also increased by several orders of magnitude the people that could be subjected to hierarchical co-ordination, the move up was also accompanied by a move to the right along the diffusion scale. Thus, treating the firm as a point in the C-space, we see it following the path described in Figure 8.5.

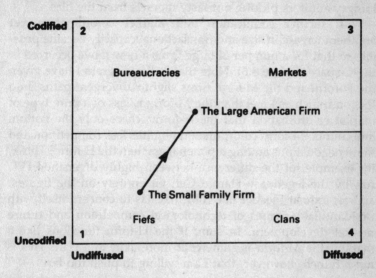

Figure 8.5 *The Growth of the Large US Firm – Phase 1.*

Yet large integrated markets, together with economic growth and the development of overseas business, continued to generate opportunities and demands that were beyond the capacity even of the large hierarchical firm. At the very top of the firm, with the introduction of the multidivisional structure, co-ordination by markets began once more to reappear but this time the market, in contrast to the one that had confronted the small family firm fifty years earlier, was *internal* to the firm and managed through the H-form. Market co-ordination requires fewer elements for effective control – return on sales, return on investment, return on assets employed, the growth of all of these – than hierarchical control where no common measures exist to allow one to compare, say, the finance function's performance with that of the marketing function. In this sense, effective market transactions, even internal ones, are more easily codified than hierarchical ones. A divisional manager submits his quarterly income statement and balance sheet and that will do. If things go wrong of course hierarchical control is not slow to reassert itself – more often than not in the form of figure hungry auditors picking out tasty morsels from the files.

With further codification and market co-ordination yet another increase in size and transactional capacity became possible so that for a number of large firms a new move occurred in the C-space (Figure 8.6). Note that in the diagram I have given the H-form and the M-form firms slightly divergent paths. I do this on hunch as I feel than the M-form is less of a pure type of market co-ordination that the H-form where only the bottom line counts. M-form co-ordination requires less competition and more negotiations among top managers than the H-form. Think, for example, of the difference between highly diversified ITT, run by the legendary Harold Geneen entirely on the figures, and an industry leader like IBM that has to concern itself with unquantifiable issues of technological competition and future market development. In sum, if the H-form functions like a market, the M-form is somewhat more akin to a clan. This is not a hunch, however, that I am willing to push too far.

The Role of Technology

Those that have followed the argument so far may be struck by the resemblance that the curve tracing the evolution of the large multi-divisional enterprise bears to the codification-diffusion curve of Figure 3.1 (p. 61). They may further find the fit between the transactional style imputed to the firm at certain stages of its growth – hence at different points in the C-space – and that which has been associated with different regions of the C-space (Chapter Five) more than coincidental.

Each move by the firm along the codification-diffusion curve was associated with changes in technology, whether external or internal to the firm: the shift from fiefs to bureaucracies went

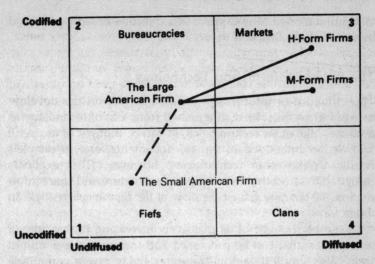

Figure 8.6 *The Growth of H-Form and M-Form Firms in the C-Space.*

hand in hand with changes in communication technology; the shift from bureaucracies to markets was facilitated by emergent data processing technologies that could chew up vast reams of well codified data. Each move was associated with a change in organization structure: from the undifferentiated family firm to the functional firm and then on to the multi-divisional firm. And finally, each move called for a change in management style: first from a personalized to an impersonalized approach; and then from a centralized to a decentralized way of achieving corporate objectives. But change the management style and you change the culture: the information that people share and the way that they do so.

Changes in technology, organization and culture each proceeded at a different pace so that it would be a brave man who could point to which necessarily was a cause and which effect. The line of causality does not affect our argument which is that their movements in the C-space were correlated. A movement in the one would have a destabilizing effect upon the others and pull it along in the C-space in a direction broadly predicted by codification-diffusion theory.

The Role of Information Technology

The influence of information technology (IT) on the development of firms must be distinguished from that of technology as a whole. Like other technologies, IT can be thought of as useful knowledge embedded in things, documents, and in people's heads. Unlike other technologies, however, IT is explicitly designed to affect the way that people structure and share information. *IT therefore acts on the shape of the diffusion curve itself.* In what way?

IT can be thought of as massively increasing the volume of information that can be processed and transmitted per unit of time. The simplest laptop computer today has a computing power which is several times greater than the largest mainframe machines of the early 1960s. Data transmission capacity has also increased. The contents of the Encyclopaedia Britannica, for example, can be electronically transmitted around the globe in the time it takes to have a brief telephone conversation.

Recall that we codify essentially for two reasons. The first is that since the human data processing apparatus is of limited capacity, we need to structure and thereby reduce the amount of data that we have to deal with per unit of time. The second is to facilitate communication; to use a communication channel is always costly in terms either of time or effort, or because its availability is limited.

IT, by preprocessing data, increases the amount of data that we can deal with per unit of time and thus reduces our need to codify. To illustrate: in order to interact effectively with a computer in the early 1960s one had to be familiar with the codes used by the machine itself, one had to master its language – the long sequence of noughts and ones in terms of which it represented the world to itself. Few people other than specialists were either willing or able to do this. Progress in computing since that time has consisted of massively increasing a machine's capacity to process and store data *and* of using some of that capacity to create higher level languages closer to the ones that we use in our daily discourse. Since the machine has now learnt to speak like us, we no longer have to master its language. We are spared the need to master a difficult code by the machines' improved data processing capacities; it has become user friendly. Today, anyone who wishes to can interact with a computer.

IT has also massively increased the volume of data that can be sent down a telecommunication channel per unit of time. Messages that had to be carefully crafted in order to fit on a telex can now be sent by fax in a scribbled form or even as a picture. At the same time the laconic one minute international telephone call is now being replaced in larger firms by videoconferencing. Thus, with enhanced data transmission, more people can be reached with more data in a given unit of time (see Figure 8.7).

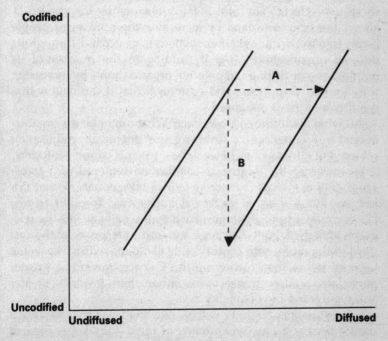

Figure 8.7 *IT Shifts the Diffusion Curve to the Right.*

An enhanced capacity to process and transmit data can be interpreted in the C-space as a rightward shift of the diffusion curve. As indicated by the two arrows in Figure 8.7, the curve shift has two quite distinct effects:

- For a given level of codification, the size of the audience that can be reached with a given message in a given period of time can be increased. This is shown by the horizontal arrow A.

- For a given size of audience, the extent to which a message needs to be codified in order to be received, understood, and effective – recall Shannon and Weaver's three level communication problem from Chapter Two – can be reduced. This is shown by the vertical arrow B.

What organizational consequences might be inferred from these two effects? The first is fairly obvious by inspection. IT allows the firm to expand by increasing the number of people it can transact with. Whether it chooses to expand through its internal organization – i.e. by adding to the number of its employees – or through its external organization – by increasing the number of suppliers and customers that it can deal with – the firm's scope is enhanced.

But what about the second effect? What might be the organizational consequences of lowering the degree of codification required of a transaction? Here, the answer is counter-intuitive.

By lowering the degree of codification required of a transaction, *a firm is in effect restoring to it an interpersonal element that had been lost as it moved up the codification scale*. In other words, IT, in contrast to technologies such as the railway and the telegraph that had built the large modern enterprise in the last third of the nineteenth century, is likely to move firms *down* the C-space rather than further *up* the C-space; towards a greater personalization of transactions rather than towards greater anonymity and impersonality.

Interestingly enough, IT will be allowing firms to move down the C-space at a time when many of them – the larger ones at any rate – are actually wanting to do so.

Conclusion

Our discussion of IT yields a more radical interpretation of enterprise evolution than that which is implicit in Figure 8.6. In that diagram, the impression is given of a linear process in which

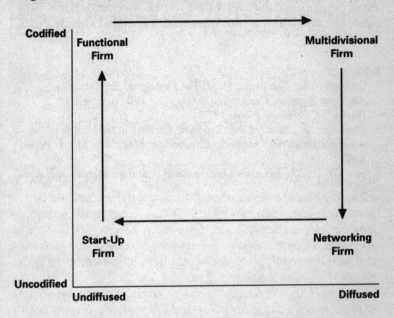

Figure 8.8 *A Cyclical Interpretation of Organizational Evolution.*

codification and diffusion interact to push a firm up and along the diffusion curve towards ever greater size. If, however, it turns out that a firm can also shift its cultural centre of gravity once more down the C-space, then a *cyclical* interpretation of organizational evolution may become more appropriate (see Figure 8.8). The evidence for such a view is still modest but growing. Some firms – Hewlett-Packard, for example – have been working hard to restore a sense of community inside their organizations. They have been tackling the problem by subdividing the firm into units much smaller and entrepreneurial than divisions; units which in their size and operating style are closer

167

to clans. Other firms – here 3M comes to mind – have allowed employees with a good idea and an entrepreneurial bent to start up their own venture with the firm's support. Such a policy in effect moves parts of the firm's internal culture to the left in the C-space, thus completing the cycle. Internal venturing or 'intrapreneurship' initiates a new round of organizational evolution, but one which is now internal to a firm that already exists.

References

1. Chandler, A., *The Visible Hand: The Managerial Revolution in American Business*, Cambridge, Mass: The Belknap Press of Harvard University Press, 1977.
2. Chandler, A., *Strategy and Structure: Chapters in the History of the American Industrial Enterprise*, Cambridge, Mass: The M.I.T. Press, 1962.
3. Franko, L., *The European Multinationals*, London: Harper and Row, 1976.

9

The Firm's External Relations in the C-Space

Introduction

If small is beautiful, then big is powerful.

The aesthetes of the management world – and many other besides – may prefer the craft-like perfectionism of the small firm, its single-minded dedication to turning out a few very fine and often innovative products, the sense of fellowship that comes from a common pursuit of this goal. This is the world of the potter, the dress designer, the small high-tech start-up. It is also the world of guild socialism, the Fabians and the anti-industry lobby.

To maintain this world in existence, paradoxically, one cannot afford to be too successful. To the product-oriented craftsman, growth is more often than not perceived as a threat rather than an opportunity, a destabilizing intrusion into his established and preferred ways of doing things – as a marxist might put it, growth introduces an alienation between the producer and his product. In such circumstances, to maintain the wholeness that comes with small size, much potentially profitable business must be turned away – often towards competitors (although these are not necessarily perceived as such) who may have other concerns.

Competitors, for example, may be concerned with issues to which the aesthete is quite indifferent: sales growth, market share, return on assets employed. The difference in objectives carries the seeds of changes in management style, in technology, and in organization. To illustrate: an increase in sales volume can suddenly allow one to make in-house at a lower cost a critical component that was bought from an outside firm. The component can now be tailor made to the firm's requirements whereas before it had to make do with something off-the-shelf. An external transaction is now *internalized*, a new machine is purchased, people are hired, and an administration system is set up since they have to be supervised; later, with three machines purchased in this way, someone is appointed to the position of full-time supervisor, a new role is therefore created, and possibly, if the expanding firm was a small one, a new level emerges in the organizational hierarchy.

With internalization, a move up the C-space is triggered off which seeks to adapt technical, structural, and cultural features of the organization to the stresses and strains of growth. Where growth and the move up the C-space is rapid, many firms find that they cannot cope. The change in values, attitudes and skills proves to be too much for them, resistances build up, and they either regress or collapse. Others, by contrast, thrive on a fast pace of change, but not without passing through a number of growing pains that may end with the departure of the founding entrepreneur. Steve Job's departure from Apple, as it shifted its attention from idiosyncratic technical wizardry to more mundane and disciplined marketing considerations, readily springs to mind as an example.

Organizational growth, which we may represent as an internalization of transactions, leads to painful changes in style. But must we conclude that organizations are required to grow in order to remain competitive? This has been the traditional, somewhat Darwinian, view of business. Firms are compelled to grow to maintain their strength in a competitive struggle where the big ones gobble up the little ones. The trick is then to become sufficiently large as to be indigestible to all but the largest competitors and then to hope that antitrust laws keep those at bay. When a predator appears in the market, the first instinct of prospective victims is to find a merger partner or to revalue existing assets – to get bigger, and fast.

Yet a growth in sales need not automatically translate into organizational growth; an increase in transactional capacity is not the same thing as an increase in organizational size – i.e. in the number of internal transactions – and therefore does not inevitably imply a change in management style. In this chapter, we shall examine the reason for this. We shall start by taking a closer look at the process of transaction internalization itself which is not the simple 'make or buy' concept that it appears to be. Then we shall try to link the process of internalization to problems of management style. This is a difficult issue to unravel and we shall only treat it here in very general terms, but it is as well to be aware of the organizational, technical and cultural complexities that underlie a firm's decision to 'make or buy', a decision usually made in the company of purchasing officers and cost accountants, usually oblivious to the less tangible consequences of their choice.

Internalization

No firm is an island. If it were, the 'make or buy' issue would not exist. A firm would manufacture everything in-house. There are indeed industrial economies where firms do try to become islands, and provide for their needs as far as possible from the inside. The People's Republic of China, to which Chapter Twelve is devoted, is a case in point. Why have Chinese firms, until recently, behaved in this way? Simply because there has been nothing out there worth buying. The environment has been too poor in resources to trust in the market mechanisms – so firms designed and manufactured their own machines, built their own buildings, constructed their own furniture, and so on.

This lack of dependency on outsiders is the antithesis of the division of labour which rests on the belief that you should make what you are best at making and buy from others what they can make better than you. What the Chinese experience shows us is that this choice is a mighty big luxury which assumes that there are others out there ready to produce what you don't feel like doing. A market assumes the ready availability of external resources – i.e. elastic supply. Where these are absent, the market fails, and resources have to be generated internally.

Thus internalization produces organizational growth in two different ways which have quite different implications:

171

- Producing what one was producing before but in larger quantities – the volume of transactions increases but not its diversity, so that specialization is maintained.

- Producing what one was not producing before at variable volumes – the diversity of transactions increases whether the volume does nor not. This leads to organization differentiation.

The second kind of internalization will likely provoke a move up the C-space and hence a change of management style before the first, even though sooner or later a change in the quantity of internal transactions also translates into a need to differentiate and hence leads to changes in their quality. We shall have more to say on this shortly.

But how does one deal with a product which is both bought in *and* at the same time made internally – what strategists call tapered integration? Or a product which is manufactured by an outside firm in which we, say, as purchasers, have a minority stake? Or again by a firm which partially owns us? In such cases, the boundary that separates the inside of the firm from the outside is a fuzzy one. Costs and benefits do not fall so neatly on either side of the boundary. It may be cheaper, for example, to purchase a machine from an arm's length supplier with whom one has no connection, but that would be taking too narrow a view of the cost of the transaction if one's future business prospects were intimately linked with the long term survival of the supplier, or if one had a substantial financial or strategic interest in the supplier's own future growth and development.

The Cost of Transacting

A useful way of looking at the internalization issue is to place the costs of transacting internally and externally along a scale. The scale might simply measure the ratio of internal transaction costs to external transaction costs as in Figure 9.1. At the end of the scale at E, where the costs of internal transactions are clearly superior to those of external transaction – i.e. where R

> 1 – the case for external transactions, that is, for 'buying in' are overwhelming. In fact, 'buying in' could only really be opposed on very compelling non-economic grounds: the need to keep a department employed until the next upturn, the loss of a critical skill, etc. At I, on the other hand, the costs of external transactions are much higher than internal ones – R < 1 – so that it is those in the firm who want to buy in that are on the defensive.

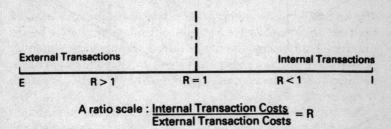

Figure 9.1 *External versus Internal Transactions.*

But between the endpoints of the scale there is a grey area in which, providing that transaction costs are sufficiently broadly defined, the decision could go either way. The size of the grey area varies with the degree of codification of a transaction, with codified well-structured transactions offering clearer cut alternatives than less codified and fuzzy ones. The sentimental attachment to a faithful supplier who knew one's father and one's grandfather before him is more likely to survive an after dinner bottle of port and a cigar than a pocket calculator.

This is a key point that can best be emphasized by placing our scale as a third dimension to the C-space (Figure 9.2). Remembering that transactions in the lower part of the space are built on face-to-face relationships and a sharing of values, and that those in the upper part are more impersonal and rational, we see that the internalization-externalization decision cannot be divorced from questions of transactional style. In the lower part of the C-space, for example, the internalization decision is fuzzier, more open to non-economic considerations. I suspect – although I cannot prove it – that for this reason it has more inertia, that it is more burdened with custom and tradition than in the upper part of the space. An alternative view could plausibly be put forward, that it is the very lack of structure in a transaction that gives it flexibility and makes it amenable to change; firm boundaries are not clearly determined and we are therefore dealing with what economists call a *quasi-*

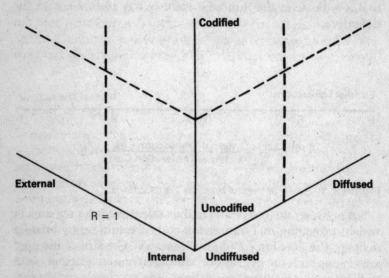

Figure 9.2 *External Transactions in the C-Space.*

firm. Only some hard-edged research could clarify the issue.

Focusing on the costs of transactions naturally leads one to ask how these costs are arrived at. This is a big question to which no exhaustive answer can be given. Should the time taken by a transaction, for instance, be counted as cost? Perhaps; but what happens if one actually has a good time on the way? Or again, how should the infrastructure that makes transacting easier – telephones, roads, computers – be reckoned in the costings? The infrastructure is a prior investment in transactions that should lower the cost of conducting them at the margin and will therefore affect both the choice of internal-external alternatives as well as the transactional style itself.

The infrastructure must be treated as transactional capital.

It comprises technical, organizational and cultural assets that influence the way people structure and exchange information. A workable and credible legal system is an example of transactional capital. By lowering the probability that when we next meet I will hold a knife to your throat, the legal system increases both the chance and the scope for mutually beneficial interaction between us. A more technological example of transactional capital is the automatic subway ticket machine that reduces both the time I have to spend in line waiting to buy a ticket and the labour costs to the transport authority of providing me with one.

Centripetal versus Centrifugal Cultures in the C-Space

Organizational examples of transactional infrastructures are provided by certain firms which, by their very nature, aim to occupy a stable position in the C-space. Such firms would lose their identity if they followed the knowledge cycle as described in the last chapter. Their organizational effectiveness requires them to maintain cultural practices whose location in the C-space is close to their cultural centre of gravity. Such firms operate what we might call *centripetal cultures*; they are to be distinguished from firms whose organizational effectiveness is predicated upon the achievement of cultural diversity, firms that will actively foster cultural practices at some distance from their cultural centre of gravity in the C-space. The latter operate *centrifugal cultures*. Figure 9.3 provides four different examples of centripetal firms and one example of a centrifugal firm. In each case the cloud of black dots represents the distribution of the firm's transactions in the C-space, with single dots representing each one transaction.

The basic mission of a centrifugal firm imposes a very strong requirement on its management style. A research firm that becomes a bureaucracy will have problems coming up with worthwhile innovations. A consultancy that becomes a fief will not long retain competent professionals. A trading company that becomes too clannish closes itself off from external market opportunities. And, finally, an engineering firm that becomes too sensitive to market considerations – whose dominant concern becomes the opportunistic 'quick buck' – will lose its technical proficiency.

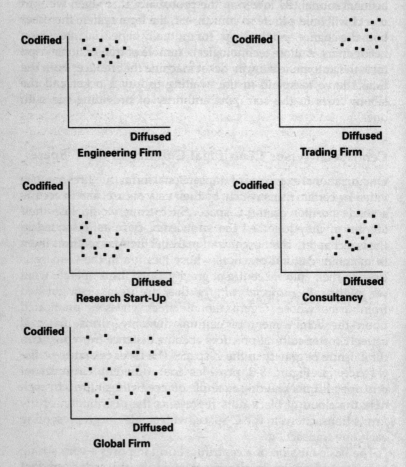

Figure 9.3 *Centripetalism and Centrifugalism in the C-Space*

Investing in transaction infrastructures is a slow, incremental business that limits the area that can be occupied in the C-space by the average firm. An old traditional firm cannot just become market-oriented overnight. The technical capacity, the attitudes, the skill have to be built up slowly by a process of trial and error. As was implied in Chapter Six, the large firm can do this more easily than the small one. Some parts of the firm will then be market oriented, others will be bureaucratic in style. Perhaps one part of the organization will end up dominating the other but, then again, perhaps not.

For the small or medium-sized firm that needs to develop transactional capacities in different parts of the C-space, but lacks the resources to invest in the appropriate organizational forms, technologies and cultures, the only viable solution is to develop external linkages with organizations and institutions that already possess such capacity. It *externalizes:* it calls in consultants to give it a strategy direction; outside distributors to sell its products; commissions contract research to come up with new products; and licenses a manufacturer to produce and sell its products. In recent years, the practice of externalization has spread to larger firms in quest of greater strategic focus and efficiency. It goes by the name of *downsizing* and reflects a growing appreciation among managers and shareholders that bigger is not invariably better.

External Transactions in the C-Space

The external transactions of the firm, no less than the internal ones, have their own information environment and thus develop distinctive institutional forms in different parts of the C-space. These are many and various and will often combine into complex packages. Figure 9.4 illustrates four types of external transaction.

Trading

External transactions in the quadrant we have labelled 'market' unsurprisingly involve buying and selling. This is a real-time competitive activity conducted between agents who may well never meet, using a few highly selected items of well codified and diffused information. Buying and selling of foreign exchange for a large bank requires a telephone, a telex, a monitor,

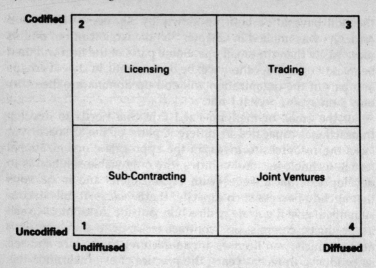

Figure 9.4 *External Transactions in the C-Space.*

and a cool head. The key skill involves juggling numbers around and knowing what they mean. Foreign currency transactions do not require a sharing of values or objectives – the deal goes to the highest or lowest bidder, not the most virtuous, or the most likeable. Ditto for the buying and selling of soya beans, wheat futures, aluminium and, as OPEC has now found to its cost, oil.

Licensing

A licence gives an outsider the right to use a product or process whose creation involved the use of knowledge in which one has a proprietary interest. Proprietary knowledge is an asset that is hard to trade in the marketplace because it is hard to price. And, once given, it loses its market value since people are usually not willing to pay for what they already know. A licence gives access to such knowledge for a flat fee but the monopolistic possession of such knowledge gives the licensor a certain power over the licensee by means of which we can impose certain conditions on the use to which such knowledge is put, as well as on how and to whom it is diffused. A licence, for example, may be granted for those markets in which the licensor does not expect to be present, but restrictions will be placed on the selling of products embodying the proprietary knowledge in question in, say, the licensor's own home market. A licence is often sought for patented knowledge, that is, codified knowledge that has been set out on paper and whose originality has been authenticated by the patenting process itself. The diffusion of such codified knowledge is then controlled by the terms on which licences are then granted. Clearly a firm's ability to control the diffusion of its proprietary knowledge depends on its ability to police and monitor its contractual agreement, yet this requirement does not necessarily imply a personalized relationship. I have seen licensing agreements established and implemented through brokers in which transferor and recipient had never met – indeed, in one case, the licensing firm was French and the licensee Filipino! The key point is that licensing is an external transaction that requires the controlled diffusion of codified knowledge, a communication condition that we find in bureaucratic transactions inside the firm. Where, among other places, are we likely to find such transactions inside the firm? In the production department, where the manufacturing steps and the product have to be specified in great detail in order to achieve targeted quality levels. A licensing agreement will often impose the same detailed requirements on a licensee.

Joint Ventures

Some transactions are too vague and uncertain for all their details to be anticipated and set down on paper. Where these involve a substantial amount of risk – the entry into an unknown market or the launching of a new product – and where one lacks the skills or resources to 'go it alone', a natural alternative is to seek out a partner with whom benefits and risks can be shared. Joint ventures are external transactions between parties who provide complementary resources in the pursuit of common risky objectives. But *are* their goals sufficiently convergent, or

179

at least compatible, to ensure the successful completion of the venture? And if something were to go disastrously wrong, in the course of implementation, would they behave like gentlemen towards each other or would one be tempted to save his hide at the expense of the other? Joint ventures, like marriage, are best entered into with people or firms that one has known beforehand. Some sharing of values, some ability to get on to the same wavelength, are the prerequisites of any long-term relationship and, where these are absent, a joint venture is doomed to a limited life. Naturally, in talking of common values and goals, I am referring to the key people in each company that will be called upon to work closely together over long periods, in fact, to the 'clan' that will be running the new organization – its top management. Hence the position occupied by joint ventures in the C-space is the same as that occupied by the corporate strategy functions in internal transacting. Joint ventures involve a looser organizational coupling between the parties to a transaction than a merger or an acquisition but a tighter one than a strategic alliance, which may involve little more than a mutual orientation.

Sub-contracting

The kind of external transaction I have in mind here does not cover sub-contracting in general but only that particular type that links large and small firms mainly in Japan but not exclusively so. The feudal nature of these transactions – characterized by longstanding, personalized, hierarchical relationships – is quite striking. Large Japanese manufacturing firms depend to a far greater extent than their western counterparts on an army of small sub-contractors for supplies of components and sometimes quite sophisticated sub-assemblies. There seems, in many cases, to be a marked preference for 'buying' rather than 'making', for the external rather than the internal transaction. The reason is not hard to see. In a business downturn it is easier to stop ordering from a sub-contractor than it is to lay off a workforce to whom one has promised a lifetime's employment and regular advancement. Japanese firms, of course, are very careful in the way that they handle sub-contractors so that the small supplier is not thrown casually onto the scrap heap, but the manufacturing flexibility offered by this kind of external transaction is nevertheless attractive. Funds that would have to be sunk into fixed assets – i.e. infrastructure for internal transactions – are released for more profitable use elsewhere. And, if informal hierarchical control of the small firm can be established from the outside, does one not achieve everything that an internal transaction has to offer, and more? Take, for example, Just-in-Time manufacturing (JIT), in which in-plant inventories are reduced to a minimum in part by carefully scheduling deliveries by outside suppliers. JIT was pioneered by Japanese firms because they could rely on the close relationships they enjoyed with many suppliers and were thus able to integrate their inputs in a co-ordinated fashion with internal operations. This could only work where outside suppliers were not in permanent competition to replace each other. The participating sub-contractor, in effect, was being offered a long-term relationship with his client. Protection and security were being traded for loyalty and compliance, the essence of the feudal transaction. A high degree of mutual trust and shared values underlie such a relationship and the manifest power that one of the parties has over the other is neither fully exploited nor codified. We shall have more to say on the Japanese firm in Chapter Eleven.

Institutions as Transactional Infrastructure

External and internal transactions, then, complement each other and allow even small or more specialized firms to respond to a variety of transactional requirements in different parts of the C-space. The small research-based enterprise can sub-contract both its manufacturing and its distribution and does not have to 'grow its own' organizational capacity across the board. The large mobile trading company does not want to immobilize assets in manufacturing operations, and therefore develops sophisticated purchasing and contracting techniques that reinforce its skills and autonomy in the market quadrant. Examples could be multiplied.

Yet external transactions need careful monitoring and controlling. They presuppose the existence of a transactional infrastructure outside the firm that does not make the whole thing too burdensome. In the upper quadrants of the C-space, for example, one might cite the existence of legal institutions that at least would enforce any existent contractual arrangements. What is the point of a penalty clause or a pricing formula that is not binding? Of a secrecy clause that does not prevent disclosure? Of a territorial restriction that does not restrict? In the lower quadrants one is looking for institutions that help to reinforce face-to-face relationships while reaffirming the common value systems that underpin them: the old school club; the alumni association; the church; the Institute of Directors; the Carlton Club; the golf club; the professional association, and so on.

The existence of these external infrastructures, or *institutions*, as we have called them, lowers the marginal cost of entering into a transaction, but only partially.[1] Part of the cost of transacting in a given part of the C-space depends on whether or not one has developed the transactional style required by that part of the space. Herein lurks a dilemma. A firm that lacks the resources to manage transactions within its own organization in a certain part of the C-space must nevertheless develop the necessary skills to handle external transactions in that region. To illustrate: a traditional engineering firm may not be marketing oriented and may use outside distributors to sell its output, but relationships with the distributor require some minimal knowledge of what customers need, what competitors are charging, or what the selling process involves. Failing such knowledge, the terms on which the transactions with distributors will occur will not be favourable to the firm so that it opens itself to exploitation through ignorance. The reverse situation can occur where a distributor buys a proprietary product, for which few substitutes exist, from a small research-based firm. The distributor may lack the industrial know-how to assess the firm's R and D and production costs so that the terms on which he accepts the product may be sub-optimal for him. He can then either lower his own margins and go for market penetration, or he can maintain his margins and sell at low volume. But in either case his profit is less than it would be if he had more technical knowledge with which to reinforce his bargaining position. Better informed, he would then be able to put pressure on his supplier to reduce his price.

Conclusion

As with internal transactions, the knowledge cycle is constantly redistributing the chips. Knowledge and know-how that were once proprietary become further codified and further diffused, and with this evolution a shift in bargaining power takes place from manufacturers to distributors, from the bureaucratic to the market quadrant. In the scanning phase of the cycle, by contrast, market knowledge may be picked up by some organizations or groups long before others, thus giving them the opportunity of acting preemptively with respect to the competition.

The knowledge cycle confronts the firm wishing to invest in its organizational assets with choices very similar to those facing a firm with respect to its technology assets – these were discussed in Chapter Seven. This is hardly a coincidence. Both organizations and technologies constitute means for accomplishing tasks at different levels of complexity; indeed, under some definitions, an organization would be considered a technology in its own right.

What options, then, are available to a firm with respect to its organizational investments? Two suggest themselves:

1 Build a dam
It can build up its existing position in the C-space and control the flow of the knowledge cycle as it passes through its internal organization. It can then invest in barriers to diffusion that enhance its bargaining power downstream. This strategy can be applied at any point in the cycle but presupposes a certain ability to monopolize cycle segments.

2 Shoot the rapids
It can follow the cycle and invest in organization so as to

allow it to do so. In this way, the small research or family firm becomes a manufacturer and later a marketing oriented firm. To be successful, it will have to adapt its own internal culture as it goes along. By the time it is through, it may well be quite unrecognizable to its founders.

Clearly, as in Chapter Seven, we are dealing with a choice between a war of position and a war of movement. Both strategies require an increase in a firm's transactional capacity but the second requires a greater investment in its growth and in the diversity of internal cultures it will be required to manage. Whether a firm chooses to grow through internal or external transactions, whether it does so by following the cycle or by staying put, will vary from industry to industry. In the field of real estate, for example, external contracting structures are well developed so that a small sophisticated team of wheeler-dealers can set up and run and own projects worth hundreds of millions of dollars. At the other extreme, a plantation will employ thousands of unskilled labourers each producing a rather modest annual output. The available technology, the preferred forms of organization, and the transactional orientation of the dominant culture will all have a bearing on the final choice. Since this mix varies across national boundaries, the choice is more complex for the international than for the national firm. To this problem we now turn.

Reference
1. North, D., *Institutions, Institutional Change and Economic Performance*, Cambridge: Cambridge University Press, 1990.

10

The Multinational Firm in
the C-Space

Introduction

Our discussion of the management applications of the Culture Space would be singularly lopsided if it did not include a chapter on those corporate Leviathans, the multinationals. One may love them or hate them. One cannot ignore them. Their operations span the globe and today they are considered key actors in the transborder flow of technology, funds, skills, and goods.

Attitudes to multinationals vary in colour and intensity according to where you live and how rich you are, and according to whether you work for government or the private sector. Some see them as the biggest threat to national sovereignty since the Roman invasion of Britain; others see them as white knights whose manifest destiny is to rescue debt-ridden Third World governments from their plight.

Rarely has so much been written by so many about so few. When taken as a percentage of total firms in an industrial economy, multinational corporations are barely visible in the final tally, yet their relative contribution to GNP and employment often dwarfs the rest of the corporate sector.

What kind of animals are these and what, if anything, makes them distinctive in the C-space? Are they just another category of large firm – in which case, there is little to add to what has already been said about large firms in Chapter Eight – or does the fact that they operate across national boundaries change the picture? In this chapter, we shall show that these firms do indeed face problems that are specific to the international business environment and that analysing them in the C-space sheds light on how they behave in coping with these problems.

We shall start by examining what is distinctive about multi-national operations. We shall then look at how the firm's trans-actional preferences are affected by dint of the fact that it operates multinationally. This will lead us to discuss the impact of host government policies on a firm's behaviour and to see how these two actors interact in the C-space.

The Multiregional versus the Multinational Firm

A firm that buys its raw materials in Malaysia, produces components in South Korea, Scotland and Brazil, assembles them into final product in Singapore, and sells them in all OECD markets, is clearly transacting in a larger population space than the firm that buys its timber in Scotland, works it up into finished products in Leeds, and then sells these in London, Manchester, Birmingham and Brighton. But then a firm operating across the United States is also transacting with a larger population than the latter. Neither the size of the space a firm is moving in, nor the numbers that it deals with can of themselves constitute the distinguishing marks of the multi-national firm. The multiregional firm also carries them. So how can we tell them apart?

Consider the difference between Figure 10.1 (a) and Figure 10.1 (b). Each represents changes in the costs of doing business – i.e. transaction costs – as a function of spatial distance. In Figure 10.1 (a) changes in costs will be mainly accounted for by the difficulty of overcoming the physical barriers associated with distance, and these are assumed to vary directly with distance – a less realistic assumption, perhaps, if you find yourself in the rain forests of central Borneo than on route 128 just outside Boston, but one which, nevertheless, will serve our purposes. Figure 10.1 (b), in contrast to Figure 10.1 (a), shows a disconti-nuity in the cost curve, a step up at point D_1 along the distance dimension. The discontinuity is not caused by physical but by the institutional and cultural changes that one meets at a national frontier – changes of law, currency, commercial prac-tice, tax level, value, habit and, above all, language. Such changes add mightily to the spatial costs of doing business at a distance and the multinational firm is one whose activities either allow it to absorb these extra transaction costs or allow it to reduce them.

We saw in Chapter Eight that US firms grew and increased their spatial reach by moving up the C-space towards a greater codification of their transactions. Multinational firms, likewise, overcome the increased costs of transacting across national boundaries by moving a greater proportion of their transactions further up the codification scale. They do this because, while both the impersonal and codified bureaucratic and market transactions can be adapted to cover a much larger and now international population through the use of telecommunications technology and standardized planning, control and reporting procedures, neither the operation of fiefs nor clans, requiring a more intimate atmosphere and frequent face-to-face interaction, can cope so readily with the sudden change of scale. The names on a company mailing list, for example, can be expanded indefinitely by simply adding memory to a desk top computer. The number of colleagues a senior executive can swap jokes with, can entertain to an informal lunch at home, or can seat in his office, cannot. Face-to-face relationships are bounded in space, time, *and memory* whereas impersonal ones are threaded together into a near infinite web that can stretch in all directions and span the centuries. Through his letters we can probably know the Roman stoic, Seneca, better than we do 90 per cent of the people who live within a two hundred yard radius of us, but who still remain stubbornly outside the reach of any face-to-face relationship.

The Process of Internationalization

Under what circumstances does a firm decide to spread itself overseas? Why would it wish to incur increased transaction costs? There are many ways that firms can get and have got involved in international operations. In some cases a foreign country is a valuable source of inputs such as raw materials or cheap labour. In others, foreign markets absorb the firm's outputs in the form of goods and services. The first kind of foreign involve-

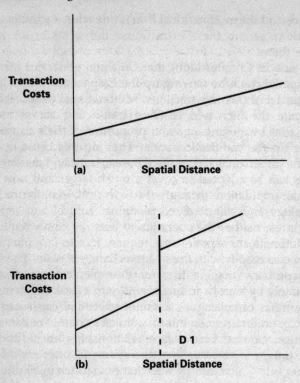

Figure 10.1 *Transaction Costs and Spatial Distance.*

ment drew European firms in the nineteenth century into colonized territories and, although it remains a significant part of multinational trade, it no longer typifies the activity of the modern multinational firm. In fact, in the post colonial era, control over domestic resources has become an important test of a sovereign government's virility when dealing with outsiders, and most multinational firms see better opportunities to exploit their comparative advantage in industrialized markets where they can sell sophisticated outputs. So without wishing to deny the existence of input oriented multinationals or to minimize their importance, we shall focus our discussion on the output or market oriented firm. How does it develop its international operations?

The typical *national* firm starts thinking of international operations only after establishing itself in its home market. The parochialism implied in such a domestic concern comes from having enough fish to fry on one's own doorstep without having to take on board the hassles of dealing with 'foreigners' (they eat garlic, don't they?). Its first contact with a foreign market will probably be a cautious one – the appointment of an agent or distributor. The complexities of shipping and documentary credits will then have to be mastered and perhaps, in some cases, instructions for consumers on the packages for its goods will need to be translated.

Such an export activity, as we have seen in the previous chapter, is an external trading transaction in the C-space. Transactions costs are modest compared with the costs of employing one's own sales force, although this is usually only true in the case of products that are simple to use. Where a product is complex, or potentially hazardous to use, the outside distributor may have to be trained and possibly monitored to ensure that the way he handles the product does not damage its brand image. This might be the case, for example, with a proprietary pharmaceutical product. For such a product, the external transaction costs could be much higher particularly in markets – typically found in less developed countries – which lack trained people and a well established transactional infrastructure. There is the further point that product complexity is a move *down* the C-space where information is less easily codified and cannot just be set down as a simple set of instructions on the packaging. Perhaps the use of the product needs to be demonstrated if its merits are to convince sceptical customers and that may call for prolonged face-to-face interaction – a considerable increase in transactional costs.

The pharmaceutical example just discussed brings out two points concerning the moves through which a firm goes international:

1 The first part of the firm to get involved in international transactions is the sales or marketing department. It is

189

located in that part of the C-space where information is the most codified and the most diffusable and thus the least costly either to acquire from or to make available to a broader international audience.

2 Providing an adequate infrastructure exists in the foreign market, these market transactions are the least costly to externalize and control. It is only when the sales potential in that market has been demonstrated through an increase in sales volume that the strategic issue of market development is posed. In effect, strategic thinking about the market requires that a marketing manager looks beyond the trading transaction itself and starts *learning* about customer characteristics, competitors, cultural habits, and so on. To do this requires a move down the C-space towards less tangible success factors than a sound selling price and ready availability of the product. In the language of our knowledge cycle, learning about his new environment requires that the marketing manager embark on the knowledge absorption phase of the knowledge cycle.

It does not always happen. All learning ultimately reduces transaction costs, but the effects of such cost reductions are both much more visible and easier to achieve in the upper part of the C-space than in the lower one. Furthermore, transaction costs themselves are much more visible when they are codified, a point which often leads firms to seriously underestimate the intangible costs of doing business abroad.

If, nevertheless, the firm does invest in the absorption phase of the knowledge cycle – i.e. a downward movement in the C-space – the moment will soon come when the marketing manager starts to wonder whether he should not replace the outside distributor with his own sales force – i.e. internalize the transaction. Why? Because if the learning acquired by moving down the C-space becomes the property of the distributor, it becomes not only more difficult to transmit back to the firm – remember it is increasingly uncodified knowledge – thereby increasing the relative costs of transacting externally for both parties, but it also increases the distributor's bargaining power in his dealings with the firm.

The Hidden Costs of Internationalization

One way of forestalling such a contingency where internalizing the transaction remains too costly, is for the firm to enter into a joint venture with the distributor in which it brings a competitive product and technical know-how and he brings an intimate knowledge of the local market and culture, as well as some potentially useful political contacts. In this way, the transaction remains external but, in following the knowledge cycle through the absorption phase, its style is modified. It ceases to be a simple arm's length trading relationship between a buyer and a seller.

In many cases this is precisely where, in international business, the trouble starts.

The lower right hand quadrant is the Achilles Heel of international business. It is the quadrant in which information, although generally available, remains intangible and hard to decode. It is here that the peculiarities of a foreign culture are hardest to discern, and the implicit values, attitudes and habits of people weigh heaviest in the transactional balance. It takes time to master the transactional style of this quadrant, to build up the shared perceptions and the trust that allow people to get on the same wavelength. It already takes time to do this *within* a culture; it takes very much longer *between* cultures. The time taken has to be considered by the foreign firm as an investment in a transactional infrastructure – a process of acculturation that requires effort and consumes resources. Any firm that would build up a long-term commitment to a foreign market, unless it is selling the most undifferentiated sort of product – and in which case what advantage does it have in investing in the first place? – must inevitably pass through this quadrant.

Yet the pressure of the bottom line, the need to show results now, more often than not blinds firms seeking out a foreign joint venture partner to the requirements of this transactional style. The tangibles are emphasized at the expense of the intangibles so that, providing a foreign partner displays both affability and competence, he will quite likely be judged suitable. In simple cases, this can work and sometimes the joint learning occurs once the joint venture has got under way – if time and profit pressures allow, of course.

But, even assuming that the joint learning is successful, at the senior managerial level of the joint venture – and what I am about to say also applies to the wholly owned foreign subsidiary – such culture-specific learning is hard to incorporate in the parent company's knowledge cycle. The cost of transacting across national boundaries has erected a hidden barrier between the joint venture subsidiary and its parent which undermines the effectiveness of scanning in the lower part of the C-space. The strategic perceptions of managers in a joint venture and those of managers located in a distant parent company can then easily get placed on divergent paths. This poses an interesting problem of strategy formulation.

The reason is set out in Figure 10.2. In the diagram, two knowledge cycles, A and B, are drawn, one representing the internal knowledge flows of the firm before the move abroad, the second representing an additional flow pattern that the firm has tapped into by internationalizing. This second cycle is flatter and more codified, indicating that outside its home base a firm will feel less able to deal with uncodified than with codified signals. A third cycle, C, indicated by a dotted line, represents the knowledge cycle that the firm eventually needs to develop if it is effectively to adapt to the local environment. It is often, however, either underinvested in or ignored altogether. Why?

Recall the difficulty of transmitting uncodified knowledge in the C-space and hence of setting up an effective scanning function. If firms find it difficult to effectively scan their domestic environment, how much more difficult is it to scan and interpret a multitude of foreign ones? It follows that the strategy formulation process, top management's key input that we earlier identified as a clan transaction, will remain much more sensitive to the intangible signals emanating from the domestic culture through knowledge cycle A, than it will to the more distant, less intelligible signals transmitted from abroad through cycle C. And the more diversified the cultures in which the firm has invested, the more complex the scanning process becomes since the various signals emanating from different cultures now act as noise with respect to the managers of each. Small wonder

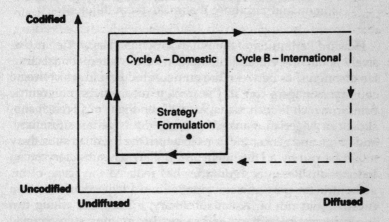

Figure 10.2 *Knowledge Cycles in the Stretched Diffusion Space.*

'foreigners' are so troublesome, and so hard to understand.

There are many ways in which this *strategic ethnocentrism*, as we shall label it, shows up in a firm's activities. I will mention only three:

- When, for example, the firm's innovation processes respond to signals emanating from the most proximate cultures – for example, when multinational pharmaceutical firms market cures for rich men's diseases in the Third World countries, soaking up scarce foreign exchange that might be put to better use.

- When senior expatriates or host country nationals are transferred back to the home country following a promotion only to discover that they are excluded from the inner circle in which strategic decisions are made because they were never around long enough to pick up the 'club rules' and get themselves 'in the know'.

- When a firm decides to develop a global strategy and to design standardized products for the world market – i.e. it aims to satisfy only those wants that men have in common and not those that make them different.

Howard Perlmutter of the Wharton School[1] has written extensively about the cultural orientation of the international firm. He distinguishes between the ethnocentric firm in which home country managers run all the foreign subsidiaries, polycentric firms in which French managers will run the firm's French subsidiary, a Nigerian manager will run the Nigerian subsidiary, and so on, and geocentric firms in which the Brazilian subsidiary might be run by a Dutchman and the French subsidiary by an Indonesian. Recently Perlmutter has reduced the scope of his geocentric category and converted it into a regiocentric one. An Asian would run an Asian subsidiary, a European would run the European subsidiary, and so on. Today, most international firms – with the possible exception of the Japanese – have moved away from Perlmutter's ethnocentric category and many seek to occupy a position somewhere between the polycentric and the regiocentric. Yet, in spite of the changes, the 'brain' of the firm, its top managers and directors, remains stubbornly ethnocentric. Indeed, it is at the base, on the shopfloor that the typical firm shows itself to be most globally minded. Does it really matter, providing that he is sufficiently trained in the manual skills required for his tasks, whether a lathe operator is Mexican, German, or Thai? But ask Rhone-Poulenc to put a Turk, a Venezuelan or a Saudi on its main board, and you will be told that the firm would have great difficulty 'fitting them in'. It was more than politics that made the Libyan stake in Fiat awkward to live with. Firms invest considerable resources in the socialization of their top managers to the firm's ways of doing business. The size of that investment increases considerably when the socialization process has to overcome cultural and national differences as well as personal ones.

In sum, as a firm internationalizes and extends its operations into new and unfamiliar environments, the clan transactions through which the upper reaches of an organization scan their environment strategically find it increasingly difficult to carry out their function effectively. By their very nature, they cannot follow the move to the right in the diffusion space that market transactions, by dint of the information they deal with, were able to effectuate. Clan transactions thus tend to remain stuck in an ill-adapted information environment and plugged into a parochial knowledge cycle. The result is a paradox. Firms move abroad when they feel capable of overcoming the increased transaction costs involved. Yet many of these costs remain hidden from view on account of the myopic scanning practices that their top management still maintain.

The Role of Host Governments

Many large firms are fully aware of the problem. Unfortunately for them, their attempts to deal with it are not made any easier by the acts and policies of host governments. These too can add to a firm's transaction costs. Quite naturally, the concern of host governments with the welfare and competitiveness of domestic firms does not always square with the needs and requirements of foreign firms that wish to invest in their country. Consider for a moment how opposed their respective bargaining objectives are. The foreign firm's main aims can be described as extracting the maximum returns from its foreign operations for a given level of investment or to minimize the resources it has to invest in a particular given country for a given level of return. What does a host government want? Exactly the opposite: to maximize the amount of resources that a foreign firm contributes and to minimize the returns that it takes out. Of course, in order to attract foreign investors at all it has to make some concessions but, as a rule, a foreign direct investment by a firm wishing to expand its operations is a more hazardous operation than an equivalent domestic investment. Not only are there often important cultural differences that it will need to overcome, and that are absent in the home country, but the external transactional infrastructure may not readily fit the firm's way of doing business – indeed, the transactional environment may be positively hostile to its presence. It might happen, for example, that the commercial ideology of the firm is out of tune with local practice so that a superior product at competitive prices butts up against a local distribution system that only works through 'connections'. Is this not precisely what American and European firms are complaining about as they try to overcome the forbidding opacity of the Japanese distribution system? Culture as a non-tariff barrier? Or again foreign legal practices may put some of the firm's contracts at risk if not its assets – as in the case of expropriation. An independent judiciary is a transactional asset that is not universally available, and it is not uncommon in a country like China, where a western type legal system is only just now being set up, to find the judge chastising and sometimes even punishing the defence lawyer for representing 'the bad guys'.

How does this affect the investing firm's transactional strategy? In two ways. Either it reduces the resources that a firm is willing to allocate to a foreign operation below what it would otherwise be so that the investment in the upper right hand market quadrant, even after allowing for risk, turns out to be insufficient to capture available opportunities. Some would argue that this describes the situation in the Chinese market today. Or, if the firm is going to commit resources, it will prefer to transfer them through internal transactions given its lack of confidence in the domestic transaction infrastructure. This of course limits the beneficial impact that such transactions could have had on the host country's economic environment. If the investor decides to have components imported from the parent company rather than having them purchased through local suppliers, then this internal transactional strategy achieves the firm's operational objectives – i.e. quality, price, delivery – at the expense of those of the host country. Of course, many factors could justify the firm's choice – a problem that Volkswagen encountered in the Czech Republic after its purchase of Skoda. Local suppliers may not be able to guarantee delivery or quality. Or, where the technology is complex or proprietary, the costs of transferring it to unqualified local suppliers may be prohibitive when an alternative is available. Finally, where a host country arbitrarily blocks the repatriation of profits, juggling around with transfer prices may be the only way in which a firm can secure any worthwhile return on its investment.

Technological Competition

A word needs to be said about the way that foreign operations can modify a firm's technological posture. Today, international competition between firms has become technological in nature, and the winners are the ones whose market performance is powered by sizeable research and development capability. Within the firm, R and D strength is expressed by a sizeable investment in the upper left hand corner of the C-space, the region in which innovations reach their maximum value through the knowledge cycle. The weakest technological position in the C-space is located in the lower right hand corner where the only skill called for is in consuming commodities, drawing upon generally available market knowledge.

Technological competition can then be depicted in the C-space as a game played along the cycle in the diagram of Figure 10.3. Those in location T are the possessors of technology. Those in location R are the recipients. Note that they are respectively located at the points of minimum and maximum entropy of Figure 4.2 (see p. 80), which are also the points of maximum and minimum value of a given technology. Possessors have two aims:

1 to stop their proprietary technology from leaking to R through the diffusion action of the knowledge cycle, and

2 to stop recipients in R from travelling to T by following the knowledge cycle or by moving upstream against it.

Recipients, as might be expected, have opposite aims:

1 to maximize the amount of leakage that flows through the cycle from T to R, and

2 to travel from R to T either by following the cycle in a 'learning by doing' fashion or by moving upstream against the cycle in a systematic policy of technology acquisition through licensing.

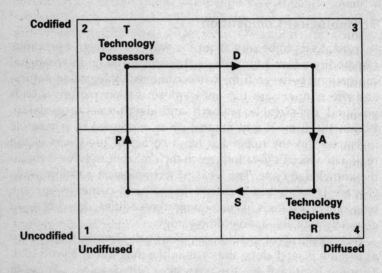

Figure 10.3 *Technological Competition in the Knowledge Cycle.*

In this scheme of things, the argument often put forward by possessors that a rapacious attitude by recipients will discourage further investment in R and D by international firms cuts no ice. For it is the *relative* position of the players that determines outcomes and not their absolute technological strength. To be technologically dominated is an uncomfortable feeling no matter how beneficial the technology. And for many technologically weak host countries national pride is an important if intangible component of GNP, even it is left out of national income accounts by economists concerned with statistical and conceptual purity.

Nevertheless, technology acquirers who are located in R and who wish to move to T face a daunting task. Not only must they master new codes, but if they are to be effective and autonomous in the use of the technology that they acquire, they must also master a good deal of the tacit knowledge that gave rise to the codes in the first place. But how are they to gain access to this tacit knowledge? By definition it is hard to codify and hence to share, which is why only a tiny proportion of it ever moves up the C-space to become diffusible. Could this possibly be the reason so much R and D work, particularly basic research – the least codified of all – tends to stay in the home country? Effective transfer can only occur between parties that both enjoy strong transactional investment in the lower left hand quadrant; failing this, they cannot get on to the right 'wavelength' and effective communication will not take place. Technology recipients in the lower right hand quadrant who try to force such a transfer – and in the case of Third World countries, I have seen several attempts – are doomed to fail.

The problem is that, all too often, technology acquisition is seen by those located at R who do not possess the technology as an arm's length market transaction in which what is purchased is co-extensive with what is seen. They are simply not aware that the technological iceberg is nine-tenths hidden under water. A cautionary tale will make the point.

I once had breakfast in Jeddah with a Frenchman who was selling food processing equipment for his firm and who had just spent a couple of days in a Saudi jail. When I asked him to explain how this had happened, he said 'I was demonstrating my milk-making machine at a technology fair. I put in some powdered milk and water at one end, switched on the electricity and, as the milk came pouring out at the other end, I started taking orders from interested customers.

'That night, I was woken up in my hotel room by two Saudi policemen who got me dressed and took me along to the local police station and there I stayed, in the local cooler – unable to understand what was going on for lack of Arabic – until the French consul came for me two days later. Only then did I discover that a Bedouin had come along at the end of my demonstration just in time to see me push the button, and the milk come pouring out. Eagerly he bought a machine. It turned out that he had no electricity, no powdered milk and no water and became quite disenchanted with his new toy. He then called the police.' A cautionary tale, I feel, for many a technology transferor.

The technological competition that I have just described is not confined to multinational firms or to international business. One also finds it at work in a firm's domestic market. What complicates things when a firm moves some of its activities overseas is that the transactional environments multiply often beyond what the firm can cope with given existing organizational resources. As Figure 10.1 illustrates, not only do they multiply but they have to be managed across a much extended diffusion dimension. Codified transactions might be able to follow, but uncodified transactions will tend to stay at home. Moreover, C-D theory suggests that even codified transactions might undergo some changes. Communication – even codified – is costly and an extension of the diffusion space will put a premium on the brevity of messages. In fact, it could be hypothesized that international operations *induce* a further increase in the extent to which messages are codified as a response to the increased diffusion requirement, a move up and across the C-space that is shown in Figure 10.4. In this way the more laconic telex message replaces the letter, and the letter in turn substitutes for the chatty phone call – a pull, in effect, in the opposite direction to the one promoted by IT. Naturally, all three are used at one time or another but the intensity with which each is used will generally favour concision and purposefulness in one's communication style.

In conclusion, we can see that a shift towards international operations will create a bias in favour of transactions in the top right hand quadrant where markets reside. The lower quadrant transaction styles – fiefs and clans – will, if our analysis is right, have problems adjusting. Will this bias towards the market quadrant, then, show up in a firm's corporate culture? And would this bias be visible in spite of IT's counterbalancing influence as discussed in Chapter Eight? This is a complex question with considerable implications for the future of international business. A proper answer will require a chapter to itself.

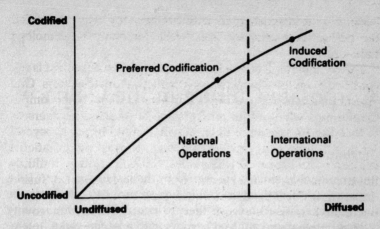

Figure 10.4 *Induced Codification in International Operations.*

Reference
1. Perlmutter, H. V., and Heenan, D. A., 'How Multinational Should Your Top Managers Be?' *Harvard Business Review*, 52 (1974), pp. 121–32.

11

Corporate Culture in the C-Space

Introduction

International business, we argued in the last chapter, creates a pressure towards further codification in order to overcome the increases in transaction costs that are incurred in communicating across national and cultural barriers with a larger, more heterogeneous population. There is a conflict here between the amount of redundancy needed in any effective act of communication for which the audience characteristics are unknown (see Chapter Two), and the concision required by limited communication budgets. Anyone who has tried to reach his Beijing representative office on the telephone from London and fallen on an incomprehending Chinese night porter will be confronting this kind of trade-off. Could it be, then, that there is some identifiable limit to how far into the market quadrant a firm's internal transactions can wander? In theory, no, since one could imagine a totally automated and impersonal transaction system in which machines talk to machines across great distances with virtually no human intervention. Thus, the factory of the future could be lost in the jungles of Sarawak for all it mattered with its operations monitored and controlled by a small two-man firm located in Bedford. Fanciful? Perhaps, but today technically within reach.

In practice, however, frail and erratic human intervention *does* set a limit to how far complex messages can be compressed into a few laconic bits. People need time to decode and interpret a condensed message, even when trained in the code and this is an irreducible cost in most transactions. The training itself is a further commitment of effort and resources. Thus, in the case of highly codified and compressed messages, what is gained in transmission time and diffusibility is frequently lost in decoding and understanding. Yet the choice does not reduce to one of communicating slowly through men or rapidly through machines, for, as we saw in Chapter Eight, advances in telecommunication technology, by vastly increasing the volume of information that can be transmitted at a given level of coding, are

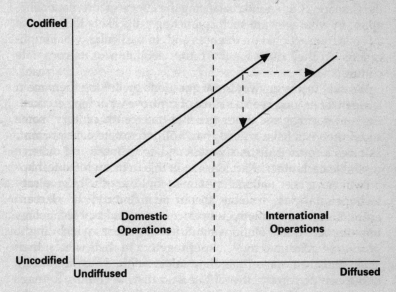

Figure 11.1 *IT Extends Communication Choices.*

shifting the diffusion curve towards the right in the C-space and opening up new choices. Combining the information of Figures 8.7 and 10.4 (see Figure 11.1) indicates what those choices might be. To be sure the bias towards further codifying transactions does not disappear. Overcoming national barriers and cultural differences remains a challenge. Yet this bias is now counterbalanced with the two quite different effects that we have identified with a rightward shift in the diffusion curve, namely, either an increase in the size of the population that can be reached for any given level of codification, or a decrease in the level of codification required to reach a population of a given size.

In sum, if the geographical extension of a firm's operations tends to push transactions *up* the C-space towards a more codified and economic communication style, the emerging technologies in the realm of telecommunications, on the other hand, by dint of the rightward shift of the diffusion curve, are either allowing transactions to extend their reach while holding their level of codification constant, or are allowing them to move *down* the C-space, thus counterbalancing the effects of internationalization. In what way are such conflicting pulls likely to influence a firm's transactional preferences and, in particular, what implications do they carry for the future evolution of its corporate culture?

We shall try to answer these questions by linking them to an issue that has long been a source of controversy among economists and sociologists. Since the mid-nineteenth century, some social theorists have argued that, with economic development, cultures lose their distinctiveness and come more and more to resemble each other. Karl Marx took this to be an historical law in which vertical national systems would gradually give way to horizontal class systems. In our own century, the Harvard economist, John Kenneth Galbraith,[1] has argued that technology imposes universal solutions on different cultures which, in the process of adapting, move closer together in their values, their style, and their way of handling information. Thus, to indulge in a touch of parody, it could be said that, in coming to terms with a McDonald's hamburger, even the French have learnt the Anglo-Saxon art of queuing.[2]

Social scientists have labelled this view of development the *convergence theory*. Its popularity seems to be inversely correlated with the performance of Japanese exports at any given time. The more submerged a country becomes in Sony video recorders, the greater the tendency to say that the Japanese are 'not like us' and are somehow 'different'. Surprisingly, this is music to many Japanese ears which, for more ethnocentric reasons, never deviated from that view. On the other hand, when Japan is buckling under an oil price rise or double digit inflation, we refer to it as a mature economy that has joined the club of those that grow at a more dignified pace – Japan then suddenly becomes a 'gentleman' and a 'chap' one can deal with. Since the case of

Japan has figured so prominently in the convergence debate, in this chapter, we shall briefly look at the corporate culture of both the Japanese firm and the American firm in order to see what light the comparison throws on the convergence question. Are they becoming more alike and, if so, in what way and in what circumstances?

Convergence as a Market Order

Our interest in convergence resides essentially in the fact that it is a theory of the top right hand quadrant of the C-space, where information and perceptions are unambiguous, well structured and shared. Market transactions rest on what people have in common. Products may be differentiated but the rules of the game, if the process is to be efficient, have to be pretty well universal in their application. Transactions on the left hand side of the C-space, by contrast, rest on differences, idiosyncratic knowledge, and asymmetrical power relations.

Convergence might be represented as a development sequence in the C-space (Figure 11.2) that normally spreads over centuries and that follows our codification-diffusion curve. Thus, for example, European culture emerged from a feudal period (fiefs) in the fifteenth and sixteenth centuries and went through an absolutist phase in which the centralized bureaucracies of the modern nation state were established (bureaucracies). Then, from the seventeenth century onwards, at different speeds in different countries, vertical transactions gradually gave way to horizontal ones as unified national markets came into being and local variants of an emerging capitalist order took root (markets).

Thus, over time, two interrelated kinds of shift take place: the first gradually moves a society's transactional options further up the C-space where face-to-face personalized forms of exchange give way to more anonymous and depersonalized forms; the second capitalizes on the possibilities for decentralization opened up by the first shift and moves transactions to the right in the C-space, towards a less particularistic and more homogeneous social order. Whether one sees the modernization

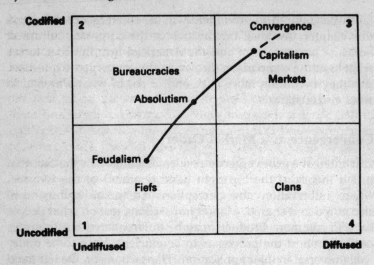

Figure 11.2 *A Liberal's View of Convergence.*

that follows these moves in the C-space as dictated by technology – i.e. transactions embedded in hardware (see Chapter Ten) – or by economics, in both cases culture gets dragged along, sometimes screaming and kicking, from quadrant to quadrant.

Proponents of convergence argue that the dynamics of modernization sooner or later makes us all like-minded so that selling a surfboard to a middle class Filipino is not essentially different from selling it to a middle class Hawaiian. In fact, the value premises of international business are today so heavily slanted towards the convergence view that the key concern of the present international economic order is to make the world a safe place for market transactions. The GATT, the World Bank, the IMF, the OECD, all take convergence theory as their implicit creed, which, of course, is not to say that they take all countries at present to be carbon copies of each other, but rather that, with development and over the longer term, they are likely to become so in important respects. This, naturally, is held to be all to the good since it allows us all to understand each other better and to get along without too much unnecessary squabbling.

Convergence has been attacked as an ethnocentric creed which allows the globe's dominant economic power, the United States, to impose its own market-based philosophy on the rest of the world. Large American multinationals occupy the market quadrant (See Chapters Eight and Ten) and so, naturally, in time, we all should. Defenders of the theory argue that the United States is the world's most advanced industrial and economic power and that it is merely pointing in the direction that we shall all in the long run have to follow.[3] Thus to try to resist the siren calls of the market quadrant is like trying to defy gravity. Convergence has the force of an historical law, and the only difference between the way that liberals and marxists interpret this law is that the liberals see the market quadrant as our ultimate destiny whereas marxists see convergence coming to a halt in the bureaucratic quadrant where a hierarchical social order can be maintained – in short, a move up the C-space towards a more codified and rational social order, but without the diffusion of information and the decentralization of power that would follow.

The apparent fit between our codification-diffusion curve and the development sequence described by convergence theory is, to say the least, thought-provoking. The dynamic sequence of our knowledge cycle appears, in part, to be consistent with the institutional shift from fiefs to bureaucracies and then finally to markets that took place in Europe over several centuries. Is this a coincidence? Or have we left something out of the picture?

Convergence and the Japanese Firm

If convergence is indeed at work, then one of its manifestations might be apparent in the organizational culture of a country which industrialized comparatively late – Japan. One would expect to see a shift of Japanese corporate culture towards the market quadrant much as it happened with the large US corporation.

However, given the still primitive state of development of the C-space as a tool of analysis, to record such a shift is a hopelessly ambitious task. Without some kind of an empirical scale for our codification and diffusion dimensions, we cannot really position a firm's centre of gravity with any precision. At best we might find good enough reason to assign firms to different quadrants so that we could distinguish between clear cases of, say, fiefs and markets and argue that a firm has more of the one than of the other. But, even so, the exercise will remain pretty impressionistic. In spite of these difficulties, I feel that the exercise is worth attempting, albeit informally, if only to assess the potential usefulness of the C-space in dealing with an international firm's cross-cultural problems. We shall therefore examine briefly a number of managerial practices that typify the large Japanese firm, contrasting them as we go along with those that prevail in the typical large American firm. At the end of the exercise, hopefully, we should get a sense of where in the C-space the Japanese firm might be assigned.

Two comments about out choice of the large firm are in order. First, the so-called Japanese management system that so fascinates western observers is largely embodied in the larger firms' practices. Small firms, to be sure, are no less Japanese, but their own way of operating reflects, and depends upon, the presence of these large firms. Our observations, therefore, although only applicable to less than a third of the Japanese labour force, describe a system that has a pervasive influence on the country's industrial culture as a whole. Second, the system that we are about to describe has been undergoing a number of slow transformations – speeded up since the recent revaluation of the yen – that we shall not take on board in our presentation. Whether such transformations could affect the analysis that follows remains to be seen.

Perhaps the best known feature of the Japanese firm outside Japan concerns its employment practices. In return for their loyalty and dedication, workers are offered secure employment and a steady progression in wages and status – that goes by the name of *nenko* – until the age of fifty-five, at which point most will either retire or be found employment in one of the firm's subsidiaries or sub-contractors. Not everyone is offered this cosy deal and the firm generally relies on a sizeable buffer of temporary workers and sub-contractors to absorb fluctuations in workload. Some of the high performers among temporary workers may eventually be absorbed into the firm's permanent labour force, and a firm will be concerned not to impose too much variation in the sub-contractors' workload – sub-contractors are seen as partners whom the firm is trying to build up over the long term. Yet the line of demarcation between an in-group with whom the firm seeks to establish a long-term commitment, and an out-group destined to absorb the shocks imposed by external conditions is a clear one and affects the culture of the enterprise as a whole.

For a start, knowing that a prospective candidate is likely to stay with you for thirty or forty years – most people are recruited into the large Japanese firm straight out of high school or university and very few are brought in in mid-career – is likely to concentrate your mind on the person as a whole. Will he fit? Does he have the right outlook? How does he spend his leisure hours? Who are his friends? Academic qualifications count probably more than they do in the west – hence the frenetic effort by parents to get their children into the right schools and the much fabled 'examination hell' that the latter are subjected to from an early age. But qualifications are only a screening device, the knowledge and proficiency they attest to not being rated very highly by the recruiting firm. In fact, the candidate on paper is only a very small part of the story. Teachers are solicited for recommendations on who would make a suitable candidate in their class and even detectives are sometimes hired to enquire discreetly into an applicant's family circumstances and lifestyle. The whole thing is much more *personalized* than would be the case in an American or European firm.

Then there is the fact that, since talented people tend to stay with one firm throughout their career, the external job market thins out fast as soon as one moves above the ranks of the semi-skilled. People who switch jobs for whatever reason are viewed with some disdain by the large firm. They tend to be penalized in their new firm with both a loss of salary *and* – very important – a loss in seniority. Naturally, then, for most, the chances of being promoted from within are rated higher *t* those of moving up by moving out. Except in the small one's organization is the only show in town. Better invest early before it's too late.

Lifetime employment has a number of very interesting consequences in practice that help to distinguish the typical large Japanese firm from its US counterpart and, for that matter, from most other western firms.

First, it makes it worth the company's while to invest in human resources development to a far greater extent than in the case of firms – mostly to be found in western countries – that risk losing their employees to competitors as soon as they have been trained. The stress on training, then, understandably has become a distinctive feature of the Japanese management style.

Second, this training, being disconnected from an external market in specialized tradeable skills, is largely specific to the firm. The important thing is that you are working for, say, Hitachi, not that you are a qualified plumber, computer programmer, or whatever. Actually, Hitachi will train you to become an all-rounder so that you can be moved from one job to another according to the changing needs of the firm. Technical change poses no threat since, if your skills become obsolete, the firm will retrain you. And the unions, being company unions and not craft based, will not stand in the way of your reassignment. You don't need a plumber's certificate, just flexibility and a broad based competence that the firm will instil into you.

The skills developed in this way are obviously more diffuse ones and more related to the 'company's way of doing things' than they are to the needs of an external labour market. As a plumber, you have more value to Hitachi than you have to a competitor because you have spent your whole working career learning the 'Hitachi way' which is not readily transplantable.

Third, the fact that people are destined to spend their working lives in face-to-face contact places a strong premium on consensus as a way of reaching decisions. Conflict becomes particularly destructive or destabilizing where people are locked in and cannot walk away. Individualism in western enterprise stems in part from the fact that if you don't like it you *can* always leave. There are plenty of other corporate fish in the sea. In Japan, the only other corporate fish worth considering are likely to be sprats – and small firms are still looked down upon by any corporate executive worth his salt – so that the penalties for walking out are likely to be high.

Decisions, then, are reached through a slow process of face-to-face negotiation that goes by the name of *nemawashi*, or root binding. It should not, however, be imagined that consensus necessarily reflects a decision that all participants are happy with. Personal power factors probably play a bigger role in Japanese decision making than they do in western enterprises and the belief that 'might is right' is never very far from the surface in Japanese culture.

Take two examples, both drawn from the firm's relations with outside institutions: the first is offered by the Ministry of International Trade and Industry's much vaunted system of 'administrative guidance' – greatly eroded in recent years, it has to be said – through which the state could 'persuade' firms to toe the government line on matters of investment and development. In many instances the State became the firm's corporate strategist. The second example concerns the relationship that exists between the large Japanese firm and a bevy of small subcontractors who depend on the company's custom for their survival. The large firm, naturally, wants them to survive, but only just, and very much on terms dictated by their own requirements. The large firm will sometimes take a large managerial involvement in a sub-contractor's activities right down to the production and quality control systems that are used and the profit margins that are set. When senior executives of the large firm retire at the age of fifty-five, quite often a niche will be found for them in a sub-contractor's organization. In this way, the personal links between large customer and small supplier are reinforced to the point where the line that separates one organization from the other becomes quite blurred.

The Internationalization of the Japanese Firm

What does our knowledge of the *international* operations of Japanese enterprise add to the picture? A few crucial features:

- Japanese firms have developed an uncanny ability to piece together disparate pieces of generally available information and use it to good advantage. Their massive imports of foreign technology through licensing agreements in the post-war years, their knack of improving on it in small steps, and then of converting it into a competitive advantage, has made them formidable competitors in the international marketplace. Note, however, that this strategy has given Japan the doubtful reputation of being a technology absorber rather than a technology diffuser. Today, even neighbouring China complains that, unlike the western enterprises that have invested in their country, Japanese firms never transfer their technology.

- Except in the sunset industries destined to be transplanted abroad, Japanese firms have been – until recently, anyway – reluctant foreign investors. The reason seems to reside partly in the difficulty of maintaining the Japanese system of management intact over large distances. Workers can be offered job security, yes; they can also be promoted somewhat more regularly than they might be in, say, an American firm. But what happens in the upper reaches of a subsidiary's management structure? Very soon, the foreign manager discovers that if he is not Japanese he doesn't rate. Without a full mastery of the Japanese language and an extensive familiarity with Japanese culture, he will never be 'one of the boys'. His career path will remain strictly horizontal. The result is likely to be a lower level of personal commitment to the organization among foreign managers than would be expected in Japan.

  Today the revaluation of the yen is putting considerable pressure on Japanese firms to invest abroad rather than export, so that the Japanese management system, 'foreign version', is likely to be modified.

- Looking from the outside in, now, towards Japan as a market for foreign goods, what do we see? An impenetrable network of small distributors tied together with Japanese manufacturers in a finely spun web of reciprocal interpersonal obligations. Your product may be perfect, your price devastatingly competitive but again if, as a foreigner, you have not invested extensively over a number of years in building up your own network of personal relationships, you just won't rate. Culture as a non-tariff barrier: inexpensive, discreet, and extremely effective.

A C-Space Interpretation of the Japanese Firm

What does all this add up to in C-space terms?

We saw that the transactional strategy of the large American firms was towards well codified, impersonal, horizontal relationships and that these supported the strong market ethos of the wider culture. The transactional strategy of the Japanese firm, by contrast, seems to favour the more diffuse, face-to-face, vertical relationship. Here again the external culture is supportive: large firms do not compete for labour; a dual labour market allows small firms to be used as buffers to absorb cyclical fluctuations; business leaders are willing to toe the government line, and so on.

What I am arguing – loosely here, somewhat more rigorously elsewhere[4] – is that the internal corporate cultures of typical large Japanese and American firms place them respectively in the fief and market quadrants in the C-space (Figure 11.3) and that, more important, they each try to maintain a position in their preferred quadrant by investing in organizational practices that will keep them there. In both cases, the external culture has developed and is able to offer a transactional infrastructure that is broadly supportive of the firm's aims. For example:

- American anti-trust laws are designed to keep US firms firmly anchored in the market quadrant and to prevent them from occupying monopolistic positions in the bureau-

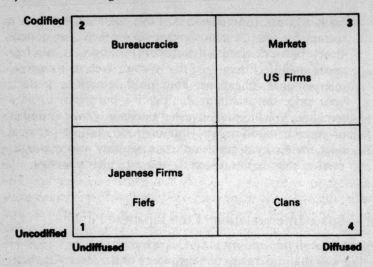

Figure 11.3 *Japanese and American Corporate Culture in the C-Space.*

cratic quadrant, or oligopolistic ones in the clan quadrant. Collusive winks and nods find little favour in a market culture. Contrast this with Japan where, in spite of the US-imposed anti-trust laws of the postwar years, the pre-war *Zaibatsus*, those large powerful industrial groupings, have re-emerged, albeit in a somewhat looser 'informal' guise.

- Most non-work satisfaction in the US – friends, holidays, family, homes, entertainment – are found outside the place of work and often in the market (with friends and family, of course, hopefully in a muted form). In Japan, on the other hand, the firm aims to take care of its workers from cradle to grave. It is not unusual to see a *kacho* (section chief) helping a subordinate to find a suitable wife, or to see groups of employees shepherded together around Europe on a firm-sponsored holiday. Friends are for the most part work colleagues, and bachelors will be invited to live in company dormitories to reinforce their sense of belongingness. To many western eyes, the Japanese company is a total institution that offers protection and security to its workforce in return for a total unconditional lifetime's commitment – *the essence of the feudal transaction*.

Nevertheless, from a convergence perspective, showing that the Japanese and US firms occupy different positions in the C-space does not, by itself, demonstrate that they are not converging and the fact that each invests to maintain a given position tells us nothing except that they like things the way they are. The thing that we really want to know is whether there is movement in the space over time and, if so, in what direction. Yet, in a sense, if over one hundred years after the Meiji Restoration and the beginnings of modernization in Japan, one can plausibly place the country in the fief quadrant, the contrast with the market-oriented American firm in fact shifts the burden of proof on to the defenders of the convergence thesis. If they argue that Japan is moving towards the market quadrant – and there are many areas where the large Japanese firm has undoubtedly developed considerable transactional skills in the market quadrant – we could still argue on the grounds of our analysis that they seem to be taking their time about it.

We could go further. We might, for instance, point out that, with their belated discovery of people management and the wide acclaim given to books such as William Ouchi's, *Theory Z*, American firms, if anything, are moving in certain areas of their operations towards a more Japanese style of management. A convergence theory in reverse, if you will, where the early modernizers emulate the late developers. An intriguing thought is that this 'reverse convergence' is likely to be greatly facilitated by the spread of information technology, to the extent that it is used to repersonalize relationships between employees in the large American firm – recall that this was one of the options opened up by a rightward shift in the diffusion curve as discussed in Chapter Eight.

But is such a 'reverse convergence', then, a move towards cultural homogeneity? Are American firms becoming more Japanese? Not a bit of it. A move towards the left in the C-space, remember, is a move towards *differentiation*, not towards sameness. Perhaps in looking at how cultures evolve, whether corporate or national ones, we have tended to place too much weight on technology as the greater leveller. Yet put a Frenchman behind the wheel of a Land-Rover and he will still drive it in a Paris traffic jam as if he were on a suicide mission rather than as a country squire. IBM and Fujitsu may be moving closer together in the C-space but it is unlikely that their employees would ever get them confused as companies. For that to happen, the move would have to occur within the market quadrant and, if it did, employees might indeed become quite indifferent as to which firm they worked for since each would have become a near-perfect substitute for the other. Employees, in turn, would have become commodities in the sense understood by Marx – also perfect substitutes for each other and, one might add, a far cry from how they are currently perceived either by IBM or by Fujitsu.

Nothing presented here amounts to a refutation of the convergence hypothesis as I have defined it. For a start, no one has ever specifically stated over what period convergence occurs – 20,000 years? 200 years? 2 hours? – and at what point the process is completed: when the whole world watches *Dallas*, munching pop corn? When a Nepalese entrepreneur invents the Sushiburger? Yet the analysis, if accepted, raises some fairly fundamental questions concerning the type of managerial practices required by economic development. In particular, it seems to suggest that, if Japanese firms have made such a success of their transactional investments in the fief quadrant, then the somewhat derogatory connotations that have grown up in the west around the term 'feudal' may on some occasions be misplaced.

Conclusion

European countries industrialized by moving out of the fief quadrant and, following the creation of a state bureaucracy, by moving into the market quadrant. Key actors within these countries developed an ideology – market capitalism – that partly matched this move and that consolidated it by treating the vestigial remains of other transactional forms as archaisms to be tolerated rather than built up. The Japanese followed a different path and industralized by moving *some* of their transactions into the market quadrant, but also – and this is the key point – by maintaining a hefty investment in the fief quadrant. They also were able to devise a modernizing ideology that spanned *both* quadrants – *wakon Gosei* (western technology, Japanese spirit). By resisting a complete evacuation of the fief quadrant, a prerequisite for convergence, the Japanese are today doing very nicely, thank you. The west is still wondering what hit it.

Will a non-converging Japan now become the new development model on which neo-convergers should focus their attention?

In the next chapter, we shall study the case of a country that is modernizing in a hurry and that is trying to repeat the Japanese trick. Only this time the country has eight times Japan's population. I refer to the People's Republic of China. What guidance can the C-space offer for its current reforms?

References
1. Galbraith, J. K., *The New Industrial State*, London: Hamish Hamilton, 1967.
2. See, for example, Levitt, T., 'The Globalization of Markets', *Harvard Business Review*, May–June, 1983.
3. This was the view defended by the American sociologist Talcott Parsons. For a similar argument in a more muted form, see Rostow, W. W., *The Stages of Economic Growth*, Cambridge: Cambridge University Press, 1960.
4. Boisot, M., 'Convergence Revisited: The Codification and Diffusion of Knowledge in a British and a Japanese Firm', *Journal of Management Studies*, 1982.

12

Managing In the People's Republic of China

Introduction

Over the last thirty-five years Japan has shown the world that there are more ways to modernize than blindly following the American or European example. To be sure, she received a helping hand from the United States after the Second World War but Japan was always very selective in what she adopted, and very reflective in how she went about adapting it to her needs. If we take the example of managerial practices, much of what passes off as Japanese management today is in fact American in origin. Yet, if corporate America dismissed the offerings of its management prophets as utopian and impractical, in Japan they found a sympathetic ear. Corporate Japan listened and then adopted, but thoughtfully, not indiscriminately. Perhaps the most distinguishing feature of Japanese management is its willingness to try something new.

Japan has become, by dint of its success, a development model for a number of Third World countries who are seeking to industrialize without losing their national or cultural identity. The stakes are high. Where a country has blindly assumed that modernization means westernization, where the old culture has been bulldozed away to make room for shiny glass skyscrapers, where the local elite pursues its studies exclusively in Cambridge, Massachusetts, or in Cambridge, England, tensions and alienation are likely to follow.

In some countries, Islamic fundamentalism will emerge as an alternative source of inspiration for the nation's destiny, in others a primitive communism will take root among the dispossessed. Clearly, if modernization has any logic to it, it is likely to be a many-splendoured thing.

One country which faces the modernization dilemma today is the People's Republic of China. With a population of 1150 million people at the last count two years ago, China houses between a fifth and a quarter of the world's population. How the country faces up to the issue of modernization, how it brings its vast impoverished population from an annual per capita income of $300 to something more in line with its fast growing Asian neighbours will have a material impact on what the world will look like twenty or thirty years hence. It is having some success. For most of the 1980s the country grew at an average rate of 9 per cent per annum, and in 1992 China was the world's fastest growing economy. Can it keep this up?

Imperial China and Japan both encountered a boisterous, expanding west in the mid-nineteenth century and in each case the experience led to an erosion of the existing order. Ultimately, each adapted in its own way by borrowing from the west – in the case of Japan, a capitalist order, in the case of China, a socialist one. Paradoxically, China, the country which had found it most difficult to come to terms with 'the foreigner', was the one whose borrowing turned out to be both the least selective and conducted on the largest scale. In 1949, it adopted a total system – the Stalinist interpretation of Marxist-Leninism – from the Soviet Union and applied it with comparatively little adaptation to its domestic culture as a whole. In contrast with Japan, which was much more concerned with integrating old and new cultural values, China wanted to get rid of its old 'feudal' order completely.

Today, the Chinese leadership has become conscious of the need for cultural adaptation. Indiscriminate borrowing is out. What is aimed for is 'Socialism with Chinese characteristics', a hybrid that will combine features of the market mechanism with more traditional central planning practices in a way that acknowledges China's own cultural traditions. The raft of reforms, first initiated in Sichuan Province in 1978 and then gradually extended to the rest of the country since then, expresses the new policy orientation. Bold yet pragmatic, they

certainly do not spell, as some have suggested, the creation of
a market capitalist order in the western and conventional sense
of the term.

Is China Converging?

In spite of an encouraging start, however, many western
observers have expressed scepticism. Either you use markets *or*
you use planning but you cannot have both. Some see the
attempt at reform as ultimately doomed to failure, a sequence
of ad hoc stop-go measures, punctuated by the occasional Tian-
anmen massacre, as the country butts up against the contradiction of trying to run two systems simultaneously. They point to
the sorry state of those other post-socialist societies, such as
Romania or Ukraine, or some of the states in Central Asia, that
are still seeking some 'middle way' between a capitalist and a
communist philosophy. Chinese are born traders, they argue,
remove the restrictions currently imposed upon them by ideology and watch them put New York in the shade in the twenty-
first century. The extraordinary economic performance of
China's two southern provinces, Guangdong and Fujian, the
ones that have travelled furthest along the capitalist road and
that today have become the least amenable to taking their orders
from Beijing, lends some point to this argument.

It is by no means obvious, however, that developments in
South China are leading to anything that we might associate
with market capitalism. Thus a key issue for China's current
reforms is to decide whether they lead to some form of convergence with western industrial economies, current ideological
and policy preferences notwithstanding, or whether the Japanese experience of modernization points to the possibility of
choosing an alternative route, more in keeping with the
country's existing cultural order.

In this chapter, I shall use the C-space to look at some of
the problems faced by Chinese state-owned enterprises as they
attempt to modernize. I shall first describe existing managerial
practices and suggest what kind of transactional strategy in the
C-space they seem to point to. Then I shall say something about

the way that the current reforms might modify this transaction strategy. I shall then conclude the chapter with a heroic attempt at interpreting the sweeping changes currently taking place in China in C-space terms. My approach will be informal and impressionistic – much of the data that I shall be drawing on was accumulated over a five-year period, from 1984 to the beginning of 1989, in which I lived and worked in Beijing. The rest has been collected since then. Much of it, however, could be interpreted in several ways. I am fully aware, therefore, that I am not going to prove anything definite and that, at best, I am painting one possible scenario for China's future development with a very broad brush.

From Planning to . . . What?

The economic institutions that China put in place after the Communists came to power in 1949 were a carbon copy of those set up in the Soviet Union. Essentially, the country was to be run like one gigantic centralized firm, with the allocation of inputs – of materials, manpower, equipment and finance – being decided for each industrial sector first at ministerial level and then gradually working its way down the administrative hierarchy, through the provincial, county, and city structures, and then down to the firm. Macroeconomic controls of industrial activity through the tax system, the money supply, and interest rates were unknown and unneeded. The all-seeing decision makers at the top of the pyramid would be the co-ordinators and the five-year plan would be their guide.

In this scheme of things, enterprise managers were not managers in the western sense of the term but rather technical administrators whose sole responsibility was to execute the detailed instructions given from on high. They would be told how much steel they were allocated, how much fuel, how much skilled labour, how many items of equipment. They would then be told, in great detail, how to use their inputs, through what kind of organizational form, and what level of salaries they were allowed to pay for what kind of work. They then had to 'fulfil the plan' and, since in most cases only a part of the promised inputs were actually ever forthcoming, plan targets had to be set sufficiently low to avoid too many red faces either at the top or at the bottom of the administrative pyramid. 'Fulfilling the plan' became something of a bureaucratic game which reflected neither the enterprise's performance nor its potential and led to many absurdities. One example will make the point. The Chinese bicycle that I own, like all Chinese bicycles, is heavier than equivalent western models. Why? Because, by using heavier steel to manufacture them, the total bicycle output reported in the plan goes up: until recently bicycle output, like computer production, was measured in tons. Simple, isn't it?

The dominant assumption of a centrally planned economy is that the vertical flow of information up and down an administrative hierarchy allows a more effective co-ordination of economic activity than horizontal flows in markets. It expresses the value aspirations of the bureaucratic quadrant in the C-space, and it will come as no surprise to those readers who recall the organizational functions inside the firm associated with this quadrant to learn that Chinese industrial enterprises are overwhelmingly production – rather than market – oriented. The main concern is with output and not with sales or profitability. Indeed, the values of the market are viewed with disdain by those hailing from the bureaucratic quadrant. Markets are 'blind' and chaotic and only serve individuals selfishly pursuing their own interest. Such attitudes are not unknown in western bureaucracies either. In China, though, they penetrate right down into the industrial enterprise. One might be tempted to conclude, on the basis of this all too brief description of the Chinese industrial system, that the typical Chinese enterprise is essentially an infrastructural transactional investment in the bureaucratic quadrant of the C-space and that, as economic performance in the former Soviet Union clearly demonstrated, such investments do not lead to the development of effective and productive managerial practices.

Such a conclusion would be over hasty. Things in China are never quite what they seem.

What is the hallmark of a well-functioning bureaucracy? According to the German sociologist, Max Weber, it is the impersonal and impartial application of a rational rule. Our own analysis of bureaucratic transactions in the C-space emphasizes the codification of behaviour through rules that allow impersonal exchanges to take place on a large scale with the diffusion of relevant information up and down a hierarchy occurring in a controlled manner dictated by task requirements.

Does this Weberian model describe the way that Chinese bureaucracy functions? Not a bit of it. For a start, *everything* in Chinese organizations depends upon personal relationships and *Quanxi* (loosely translated as personal influence). What you can do turns on who you know. Second, the rules are not generally the outcome of a rational deliberative process, as Max Weber prescribes it, that looks to how they work out in practice but, in many cases, merely the expression of personal will and preference. Rules ebb and flow according to season and circumstance. Most Chinese know this and simply wait for the seasons to pass. In any event, the rule is usually so vaguely formulated as to allow an almost infinite number of interpretations and, conveniently, much gets lost in the translation as it travels up and down the administrative hierarchy.

To be sure, relationships in Chinese culture are intensely hierarchical, but they are not of the impersonal kind that one associates, following Weber, with modern bureaucracy. There is nothing Kafkaesque about Chinese bureaucracy. Rather the relationships are of the personalized hierarchical kind that characterize feudal transaction. In C-space terms, what we actually have are fiefs hiding inside an ill-fitting bureaucratic structure. Most outsiders see the external structure and conclude that what China suffers from is too much bureaucracy. They are wrong. *China suffers from not having enough bureaucracy*. A closer look at the current reforms will show us why.

At the death of Mao, the new Chinese leadership had set the country an ambitious goal by any standard: to quadruple GNP in the twenty years between 1980 and the year 2000. To achieve such a target, they recognized that the central planning mechanism had to be changed since, under the system that then prevailed, enterprises had neither the resources nor the incentives to improve their performance. The changes announced on 20

October 1984 aimed specifically at state-owned enterprises – collective and family businesses, to their great advantage, were more or less ignored – were only the first in a long series of measures that were designed over the next few years to transform the Chinese industrial landscape. The key ones can be summarized briefly.

They aimed to:

1 Give enterprises more responsibility for their own profits and losses. Until then all profits had gone to the state and all losses were covered by the state. Providing an enterprise did what it was told, financial performance was not its concern. Now the bonuses paid by enterprises to their workforce would be linked to their profits. The bonuses in state-owned firms were never princely, but then neither were wages and, in many cases, under the new dispensation the bonus paid could equal up to four months' wages.

2 Reduce the role of central planning in deciding production levels and orientation. In a number of state-owned enterprises that I worked with, state quotas, even in the mid 1980s, had been reduced to less than 30 per cent of total output. Today, save in a few key industries, planning targets have virtually been abandoned. The enterprise is still expected to produce certain categories of products – a constraint that deprives it of much strategic flexibility – but it can decide for itself in what volume to produce these as well as where and how to distribute them. Formerly, all its output went to state wholesalers.

3 Reduce the role of the Communist Party in day-to-day management. A number of enterprises in the 1980s had moved over to what became known as the 'director responsibility system' in which the general manager of the firm was given the power to make a number of key decisions concerning the firm's basic orientation. These had been the sole prerogative of the enterprise's party committee.

4 Maintain a clear distinction between the administrative

decisions of the state and the managerial decisions of the enterprise. Fiscal reforms have substituted a corporate tax levied on enterprise profits for the old practice of just handing over all profits. Once the enterprises have paid their taxes to the state, they can use the remainder for distribution as bonuses, for welfare expenditures on the workforce, or for investment. Although the amounts involved have typically been quite modest, they have had a strong impact on the behaviour of enterprise employees – not always in the direction intended by the reforms.

5 Promote a horizontal rather than a vertical set of economic relationships characteristic of markets. This last measure is strongly linked to attempts at reforming the price system. In certain sectors, and within a certain range, enterprises were now free to set their own prices. The idea was to encourage firms to respond to price signals coming from 'out there' in the market, rather than to instructions coming from on high, in the industrial bureaux or ministries. Another kind of horizontal relationship was built up with banks that were destined to have a much larger role in the financing of enterprises, gradually replacing the state subsidies on which most firms had depended.

None of these reforms is about to usher in the golden age of Chinese capitalism. Nor were they intended to, as the leadership has repeatedly made clear. But they have already injected a dynamism into the Chinese economy which some old party cadres view with the deepest foreboding, and the younger ones find hard to control or even to understand. In some areas things have considerably improved following the reforms, although in others resistance and much corruption have taken root. But we are not here interested in passing judgement which in any case would be premature. The question before us, following our earlier discussion, is whether the problems faced by Chinese state-owned enterprises as they move, albeit cautiously, part of their transactions towards the market, are those we would associate with bureaucracies or fiefs. No clear answer can be given to this question since to some extent both are involved; yet, if we now try to assess progress registered by the reforms just cited, we come up with findings which are, to say the least, suggestive. Taking them each in turn:

1 Giving enterprises responsibility for their profits and losses only makes sense where profits and losses are valid measures of enterprise performance. In China, however, where the price of many inputs, such as raw materials and labour and, in producer goods industries, much of final production is still set by the state, and where the volume produced and the equipment used is still not under the enterprise's control, profit measures the quality of an enterprise's 'relationships' – with the planning or labour bureaux, or with the city administration – far more than it measures solid industrial performance. Finding a valid external measure of overall enterprise performance for the time being remains elusive. The same thing goes for internal measures of enterprise performance where loose and ad hoc accounting practices mean that the evaluation of a worker or a department can still be a pretty subjective, not to say arbitrary, affair. The bonuses given to workers tend therefore to be distributed on an egalitarian basis for the most part and thus contribute little to motivating performance. In sum, the absence of workable formal accounting systems inside the enterprise, or of well codified price signals outside the enterprise, makes it hard to evaluate a state-owned enterprise's past performance or its future potential. The enterprises that get ahead are the ones that build up their connections, not necessarily their performance.

2 In spite of planning quota reductions in the enterprises' activities, the influence of the supervising bureau on enterprise activity remains very strong. A city administration, for example, may decide to build up certain enterprises in certain sectors and to allocate scarce investment funds to the purchase of foreign equipment and to the development

of certain products. Competition between firms here is then not so much for customers in a market as for sponsors in an administration. Today the state-owned sector in China is in crisis with many firms losing market share to smaller, more nimble-footed collective enterprises and family businesses. Perhaps as many as two thirds of state-owned firms are making losses and only survive on subsidies. Unsurprisingly, investment funds have become somewhat scarce for these firms which still depend on the bureaux of the city or provincial administrations to finance their expansion in whole or in part. The plan may play less of a role in enterprise activity but the bureaus which administer the plan retain much of their primacy. So how do bureaus allocate scarce investment resources? Clearly they can only partially rely on enterprise performance measures since these are so unreliable. The answer is still, to a large extent, 'relationships'.

3 The director under the 'director responsibility system' is responsible for production and technical matters, and the party committee is responsible for ideological and personnel matters. Recent experience suggests that an enterprise's performance, to some extent, depends on the quality of the relationship between enterprise director and party secretary. Nevertheless, the net result of this dual leadership is that the enterprise is trying to optimize a much more diffuse set of goals than a western firm does. If the director wants to reinvest profits, the party secretary may want to build housing for the firm's employees or a school for their children. In a sense, the Chinese enterprise behaves like the small family-owned firm; it aims for a good enough performance rather than an optimal one. Workers will not want to be pushed too hard and, given the small rewards for effort, a 'quiet life' becomes an attractive alternative. As with the Japanese firm, the workers are a far more important constituency for enterprise managers than the shareholders – in this case, the state.

4 The horizontal relationships that are so eagerly sought are being undermined by the lack of any communication infra-

structure on which they can be built up, as well as by the protectionist policies of cities seeking to protect 'their' enterprises from outside competition. As a World Bank report on China pointed out, the country has a rural road network that is less than half that of India's and a totally antiquated and overloaded railway network. Yet regional protectionism is in fact a much more serious issue. A fifteenth century Florentine would feel quite at home in the city states of China which Mao Zedong himself once described as 'kingdoms within kingdoms'. Since the city and provincial authorities depend upon their enterprises for the provision of schools, housing, health facilities, and taxes, they do not wish to see them threatened by outside competitors, and will go to great lengths to keep out competing products from neighbouring provinces. One example will make the point: a textile mill in one of the southern provinces used to get its dyeing and printing done outside the province because it could not get a satisfactory level of service and quality locally. The provincial government 'instructed' the textile mill to sub-contract these tasks inside the province with the result that the mill's sales dropped dramatically in the following year.

The above discussion points to an interesting – and hopefully, by now, familiar – relationship that continues to bind an enterprise to a given locality. Enterprises, in effect, are offered protection by their cities or provinces in return for loyalty – the essence of the feudal relationship. If transactions *inside* the enterprise are personalized and hierarchical for lack of any well codified management systems, the same is true for relationships formed between the enterprise and outside institutions – bureaux, suppliers, customers – where the absence of well codified market signals or of any supporting communication infrastructure tends to bias transactions towards the local and the familiar.

The result is a constant tendency for the social and economic fabric to fragment into local fiefs that seek self-sufficiency and that remain stubbornly inward-looking. In contrast to the private sector which today appears to be growing uncontrollably, much of China's state-owned sector appears to be trapped in this 'Iron Law of Fiefs'.[1] How might this be interpreted in the C-space?

China's Modernization in the C-Space

Consider the situation as described in Figure 12.1. The rightward pointing arrow starts in the fief quadrant and lands in the clan quadrant. This is what results from any attempt at decentralization in the absence of viable infrastructure. Decentralization needs a minimum of hierarchy if it is to cope with larger numbers than can be handled face to face. Without some hierarchical regulation, markets can indeed become blind and exploitative. Remember that European countries only successfully decentralized into the market quadrant from the bureaucratic quadrant following the institutional creation of the strong centralized state.

But, it might be countered, has China not always been a strong centralized state? What about the fabled imperial bureaucracy of former times? My reply will be a cautious one, for I am not a Sinologist, but I will begin by noting that the imperial examination system, for all its importance, often did not produce many more successful candidates in any one year than the seventy students being produced by the MBA programme that I directed for five years, first in the Chinese State Economic Commission and then later in the Commission for the Reform of the Economic Structure. The lack of institutional alternatives to the state bureaucracy has blinded us to the fact that it was little more than a pimple on a vast Confucian social fabric that served to underpin it and give it legitimacy. Confucianism might well be described as the ethical order of the fief quadrant, with its emphasis on personal virtue, leadership by personal example, and filial piety.

When the Communists came to power, they defined their task as doing away with what they saw as the prevailing feudal order and replacing it with a Marxist-Leninist system – an ambitious thrust away from the fief and towards the bureaucratic quadrant (Figure 12.2). As it turned out, they successfully replicated the

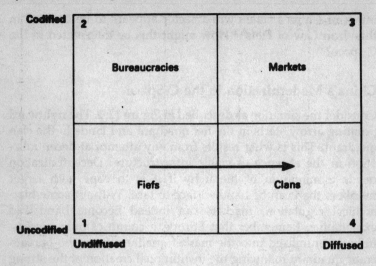

Figure 12.1 *Fragmenting the Social Structure through Premature Decentralization.*

outward *form* of a bureaucratic transactional style, but ultimately failed to grasp the nature of its inner *content*. The structure that they subsequently built up projected an image of strong central state power that did not really correspond to the highly parochial, informal and personal way that day-to-day business is actually conducted in China. Russia, in its post-socialist phase, is also discovering that its now discarded Marxist-Leninist order was but the visible bureaucratic tip of a vast feudalistic iceberg.

If this tentative diagnosis is halfway right, then the conclusion, although obvious in C-space terms, is quite counterintuitive for anyone used to stereotyping communist regimes as inflexible monoliths. China needs *more* bureaucracy and not less if its enterprise reforms and its moves towards market transactions are going to succeed. Not the bureaucracy of the power hungry apparatchik, ruthlessly and capriciously exploiting his position in a vestigial feudalism, but the rational application of impersonal rule conducted in such a way that, first, delegation

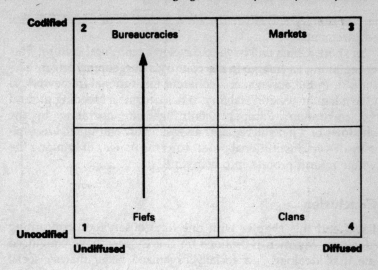

Figure 12.2 *The PRC's Early Modernization Strategy.*

from the centre to the periphery can create a stable framework for the development of a uniform administration and, second, in some areas decentralization can gradually take over from delegation when tested administrative mechanisms exist to handle the mostly self-regulating nature of market transactions.

The alert reader will be aware by now that our prescription for China, in one important respect, stands at odds with our observations concerning Japan. Did we not after all argue that Japan modernized in the fief quadrant? Why then should China not do likewise? Why is it being asked to move towards bureaucracy? The contradiction is only apparent, for we are not saying – as many Chinese intellectuals seem to be saying – that the country should evacuate the fief quadrant completely. The transactional styles offered by different quadrants are not exclusive alternatives in a complex society, they are necessary complements. Just as a firm will find one organizational sub-culture (e.g., R and D) located in the fief quadrant and another (e.g., Sales) located in the market quadrant, so the wider culture will have to diversify its transactional investments in order to create an appropriate infrastructure for a variety of new and complex requirements.

In short, China will have to develop a *centrifugal* culture. This is beginning to emerge in the country's burgeoning private sector but, in the absence of a coherent institutional framework to give it legitimacy and stability, it has become a breeding ground for corruption. Rampant centrifugalism, operating in the shadows of what still remains an essentially *centripetal*, ideologically driven, institutional order, runs the danger of bringing the whole reform process into disrepute.

Conclusion

I will end this chapter with one final observation concerning ideology. My own reflections on the C-space have convinced me that ideology is a socially organized belief that *all* social transactions and their appropriate institutional forms should be confined to a particular region of the C-space – Figure 12.3 gives an example of some ideologies associated with given quadrants. Ideology, then, tends to exclude transactions in quadrants whose value systems are perceived as a threat to its own. For example, the self-seeking behaviour of market transactions threatens the disinterested benevolence of a Confucian order, and vice versa. Ideologies rest upon particular concepts of man. Alternative concepts sap their very foundations. At the end of the 1960s, the sociologist, Daniel Bell, was proclaiming the end of ideology. In one sense he was wrong, for ideology is still with us. If you doubt it, peruse any daily paper and count up the number of conflicts worldwide which remain ideologically motivated. But, in another sense, he was right, for the hegemonist tendencies of a centripetal ideology in the C-space have today become incompatible with the needs of a complex society. Only a centrifugal cultural order can cope with complexity; only a centrifugal cultural order can lead to modernization.

If socialism with Chinese characteristics is to succeed, it will have to build up a stronger transactional capacity in the bureaucratic quadrant, but it will also simultaneously have to build up transactional skills in *all* the quadrants. Having once

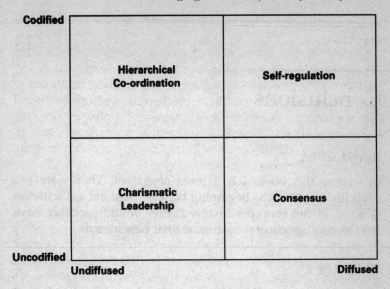

Figure 12.3 *Different Ideologies in the C-Space.*

successfully invested in the bureaucratic quadrant, the country cannot then afford to ensconce itself there centripetally in the name of ideology. It is to the current leadership's credit that it has realized this.

Reference
1. For a discussion of this 'law' see Boisot, M., and Child, J., 'The Iron Law of Fiefs: Bureaucratic Failure and the Problems of Governance in the Chinese Economic Reforms', *Administrative Science Quarterly*, December 1988.

13

Conclusions

Introduction

In writing this book, I had three objectives. They were not explicitly stated at the beginning because, without a discussion of some of the concepts involved, they would probably have left the unsuspecting reader somewhat bewildered.

Objective 1

The age of the energy based economy in advanced industrialized societies is drawing to a close. When the selling price of the software that drives a personal computer exceeds that of the hardware that makes up the computer, one can reasonably suppose that the age of information is taking over. My first objective, therefore, was to sketch out in a simple and accessible outline *a political economy of information* consistent with its new role as the key resource in a modern competitive economy.

Objective 2

Conscious as I have been that, in the last ten years, cultural issues have become a dominant concern of managers, whether they are focusing on the firm's internal processes or on its relationships with an external environment, my second objective was to show that a political economy of information and a theory of cultural processes *were in fact one and the same thing.*

Objective 3

Having provided some theoretical underpinning that would justify a manager's concern with cultural processes, my third objective was to spell out in a tentative way some of the applications
that the concepts presented might find in his work.

Assessment

This book is not a heavy theoretical treatise. Nor is it a popularized version of a body of obscure concepts accessible only to
the initiates. The theory of Codification and Diffusion is in
essence what has been presented in these pages. Naturally, I
am aware of the simplifying assumptions that I have been led
to make in order to keep things clear and of the many qualifications that would weigh down a more academic work. Yet, if
these ideas have any value – and this can only be tested out by
gradually transforming the C-space into a usable managerial
tool – then they will survive the inevitable modifications and
refinements through which the real world reasserts itself when
dealing with theories that claim to simplify it. In this sense, a
new concept can be likened to a new product: no amount of
laboratory experimenting will replace a real market test. Of
course, where a product might be toxic, laboratory testing is
essential, and in the realm of ideas safeguards are also sometimes needed to prevent intellectual casualties. But no one, I
hope, is likely to be hospitalized after coming into contact with
the Codification-Diffusion bug. My hope, of course, is that it is
contagious. My assumption, however, is that it is not harmful.
Early applications of the theory in a company context – to problems of internal culture, of technology, of strategy – suggest, if
anything, the contrary. It creates among managers a common
language to talk about things that are usually intuitively felt but
hard to articulate.

Objective 1

The move from an agrarian to an industrial economy required people to rethink the meaning of wealth. It was no longer thought to be embodied exclusively in land but, in the age of the merchant, in gold and silver, and then later, with the appearance of the industrial entrepreneur, in capital. Thus the conditions required for the production and sharing of wealth underwent a profound transformation in the course of the sixteenth, seventeenth and eighteenth centuries. Today a similar shift is taking place with the appearance of information as the new embodiment of wealth. A political economy of information therefore must concern itself with the conditions under which information is produced (codified) and shared (diffused).

Codification-Diffusion theory explores both the physical and technical properties of information itself and the circumstances under which it is produced and exchanged – the transactional strategies to which those properties give rise. Thus, inevitably, C-D theory has implications for political economy as we have defined it.

Information is a strange animal. As we have already seen, the costs of reproducing it are a tiny fraction of the costs of producing it in the first place. This is not true of capital. To be sure, the cost of the thousandth machine in a production run will be substantially lower than the cost of the first but the drop in costs will be nothing as dramatic as that which occurs when information is reproduced. The cost of producing a twenty-page Nobel prize-winning scientific paper is measured in man years; the cost of reproducing it is measured in cents *from the second copy onwards*.

Thus although the *utility* of information is maintained with diffusion – a Nobel prize-winning paper remains useful, no matter how many people read it – its *value*, measured by what people are prepared to pay to read it, very quickly drops to nothing as soon as it becomes easily reproducible. Like the air we breathe, it becomes a free good unless barriers to its diffusion are set up in good time. The great paradox of information is that it is costly to produce (codify) yet as soon as it exists in a structured form it simultaneously becomes reproducible and thereby stands to lose much of its value. Conventional economic analysis has not been able to handle such manic depreciation of an economic resource.

It is only when the dynamic properties of information, in particular the cyclical flow of new information as it evolves, have been mapped out in the C-space that the conditions of information production and exchange become apparent and that the transactional strategies of possessors and seekers after information can be studied. Conventional economic theory can only take us part of the way since it has developed analytical tools whose scope is largely confined to the market quadrant. In all other quadrants, they invoke 'market failure' as an excuse and hand over to sociologists or organizational specialists. Yet the production and exchange of information goes on throughout the C-space both within *and between* organizations. A political economy of information cannot therefore confine its interests exclusively to the market quadrant. That would be parochial. Fortunately, some economists, most notably Oliver Williamson[1] are aware of the challenge that information poses for their discipline and are adopting some novel approaches.

The key characteristic of information as an economic resource resides in its much greater mobility than alternatives. Codification-Diffusion theory explores the circumstances under which such mobility will be activated, and to whose advantage. Crudely summarized, agricultural wealth moved on carts from the fields into the local towns, capital could move by rail or ship between major industrial centres, information moves globally and instantaneously across the airwaves. How many people, I wonder, sensed the power of this new form of wealth when they contemplated the pictures of Halley's Comet relayed back to Earth in a matter of seconds by the space probe Giotto in March 1986?

Yet it is the very mobility of information that renders it so intractable for economic analysis, for it is hard to control and therefore hard to appropriate. If ownership of the means of production is the hallmark of the capitalist order, such ownership becomes critically unstable when the means of production are codified information. One only has to look at the rate at which high tech firms in, say, the electronics industry are liquidating their information assets to see how an accelerating knowledge cycle can undermine the ownership of information resources. The only way to slow down the mobility of information is to keep it uncodified in people's heads. But this only changes the nature of the appropriability problem, it does not eliminate it. When 'the brains walk out of the door', a firm's information assets often walk out with them. And even when they do not walk out of the door, whose property are they? Can property rights in something as fungible as information ever be fully enforceable?

In sum, a description of the behaviour of information in the C-space identifies some of the key variables on which a political economy of information might be built.

Objective 2

If a political economy of information is essentially concerned with its production (codification) and exchange (diffusion), then it follows from our earlier definition of culture as the structuring (codification) and sharing (diffusion) of information, that we are most likely dealing with the same phenomena. What is then left to do is to show how the transactional strategies of actors in the C-space – responses to local conditions of information production and exchange in the space – gradually crystallize into stable institutional forms that express an interplay of values, beliefs and attitudes consistent with the chosen strategies.

It is only when transactional strategies repeat themselves or where the values they express or challenge are critical to the social order that institutionalization becomes economically worthwhile. Institutions, much like the organizations through which they operate, are social infrastructural investments designed to lower the cost of promoting or of containing transactions in a given region of the C-space.

Sometimes institutions in different parts of the space mutually reinforce each other, sometimes they are in opposition. Parliament, the British Civil Service, the Carlton Club, and the merchant banks of the City of London, for example, would all be assigned to different regions of the C-space, yet together they reinforce a particular sub-culture known as the Establishment (Figure 13.1). Yet if we transplanted this cosy arrangement to Italy and replaced the Carlton Club with the Mafia – a clan par excellence – we would get the negative and debilitating relationships of Figure 13.2.

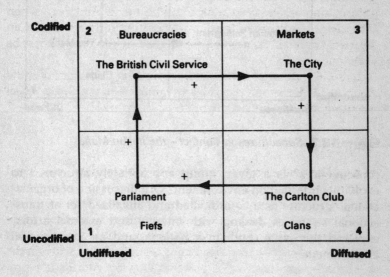

Figure 13.1 *The Self-Reinforcing Nature of the British Establishment in the C-Space.*

Culture in the C-space – whether taken at the level of a single organization or of a whole nation – is an institutional *pattern* of transactional strategies. The pattern may be well integrated or fragmented, highly productive or destructive, or both. A fully developed political economy of information should be able to assess the fitness of a given institutional pattern for a given information environment. Does it stimulate or hinder the flow of knowledge through the cycle? Does a particular clan behave like a market? Is there a lack of institutional investment in one region of the C-space and, if so, what are the reasons or the

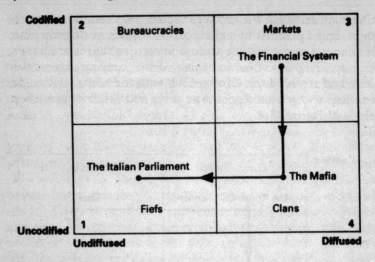

Figure 13.2 *Subcultures in Conflict – the Italian Mafia.*

consequences? Is a given group appropriately structured to exploit its information environment? Our discussion of organizational structure as a co-ordinated and stabilized set of transactional strategies dealing with internal and external actors, explored this issue, both in a national and an international environment.

Objective 3

At the level of the enterprise, the problem of 'fit' between a firm's transactional strategies and its information environment becomes a critical challenge for the manager. How well, they might ask, does their firm's internal culture integrate the firm's knowledge assets as embodied in its technologies, organizational practices, or stock of skills? How well does this internal culture cope with external information environments and institutions?

In our examination of the Japanese enterprise, we have only been able to sketch out the barest outlines of some possible answers to these questions. Our subsequent discussion of

Chinese enterprise reforms was vaguer still. Yet, in both cases, the C-space pointed to some promising lines of development. It might be possible, with some firming up of C-space analysis, to use it at different levels of resolution, focusing successively on a firm's technology, its organization, its culture, and its wider environment. What constitutes a good 'fit' between those elements at present can only be grasped intuitively. A more durable answer will need further research.

My hope, however, is that our analysis will have brought home to the reader the extent to which the field of corporate culture is in need of theoretical underpinning. Contrary to what has been claimed by some, it cannot be reduced to the driving vision of a founding entrepreneur, the cathartic effects of the company song, or the lapidary inscriptions of the corporate charter. These elements *may* turn out to be necessary components of such a culture and may help to integrate it, but they are far from being the whole story.

A further development of the C-space as a usable tool in the hands of a manager should allow him to anticipate certain types of technical and organizational developments within his firm. Suppose, for a moment, that he is running a small Silicon Valley start-up. An understanding of the knowledge cycle would allow him to foresee that the entrepreneurial, charismatic fief that he currently operates will sooner or later be replaced by the larger, more bureaucratic organization. Should he try to remain a fief? Or should he ride with the tide and adapt his organization to the demands of a new segment of the cycle? He must make a choice. If he opts for the fief quadrant, because that is the kind of life he enjoys, then he must learn to let go of promising technologies and products, allowing them to be taken over by others. If he wants to hold on to them – and this is usually the temptation – then he must develop the more impersonal hierarchical style of the bureaucratic quadrant. Of course, he could invest in both quadrants if his resources allow it. Yet what he cannot afford to do is to run them both with either a fief or a bureaucratic managerial style. Alas, this is a lesson that many entrepreneurs seem to find hard to learn. But nor does it come easily to large bureaucratic empires which seek to diversify their operations by buying into fiefs and then try to run them as if they were just another department. Exxon's experience with Zilog is a salutary reminder that even the bureaucratic style has its limits.

Looking Ahead

In these pages, I have held back from some of the wilder speculations which reflections on the C-space might invite and some of my readers may feel that what has been presented is speculative enough as it stands. Yet, in these concluding paragraphs, I would like to take the willing reader outside the field of management and allow him to glimpse at new pastures in which Codification-Diffusion theory might one day be found grazing.

The knowledge cycle describes a process of social learning in which a scanning activity collects stimuli from the environment and diffusion represents a response. Where the cycle is flat and located in the upper region of the C-space, we are close to the kind of learning described by conventional behaviourist theories that use stimulus-response (S-R) models (Figure 13.3), but, where the cycle traverses the whole C-space, it becomes a gigantic feedback loop that now incorporates the fermentation of experience (absorption) and creativity (codification) as constituent parts of the learning process (Figure 13.4).

We have so far used the vertical dimension of the C-space to describe the kind of information structuring that goes on within an individual mind and the horizontal dimension to describe communicative activities that take place between minds at various levels of grouping – sub-units within an organization, an organization as a whole, or groups of organizations. The question that one might now wish to ask is whether or not the theory of information structuring and sharing has application at a more fundamental level, say, that of a biological organism. Our discussion of evolutionary production functions in the introduction suggests that the question may not be completely meaningless.

That individual organisms of whatever species develop communication strategies is now well established, whether these take the form of mating calls, courtship dances, or territorial

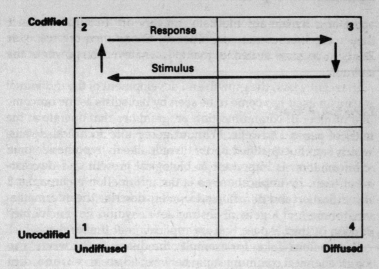

Figure 13.3 *A 'Behaviourist' Cycle in the C-Space.*

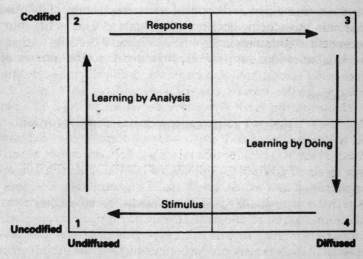

Figure 13.4 *The Knowledge Cycle as a Learning Process.*

claims. Such strategies lack the plasticity and scope of human speech and gesture and are, for the most part, 'wired in'. The sight of a female automatically triggers off a courtship dance under specified conditions, whereas among men the response tends to be more muted and varied, whatever the power of the drive.

In recent years, the growth and development of the individual organism itself has come to be seen by biologists as the outcome of a number of communication programmes that operate at the level of genes and cells. Without going into technical details, which I am not qualified to do, I would like to hypothesize that, if information is important to biological growth and development then, by implication, so is the information environment. If codification and diffusion adequately describe the information environment at a general abstract level, would not an adapted version of the C-space find an application at the level at which cells function? Take, for example, the difference between 'analogue' chemical communication between adjacent cells and 'digital' electrical communication along nerve fibres. Do they not correspond in some way to the distinction we have drawn between uncodified and codified messages (Figure 13.5)? And where in this scheme does one place hormonal communication or genetic communication?

Such questions appear at first sight to be eminently

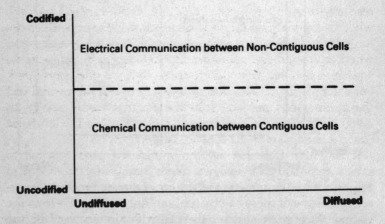

Figure 13.5 *Communication at the Cellular Level.*

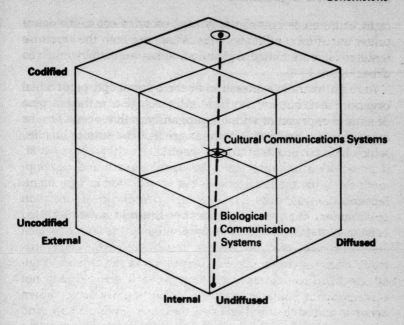

Figure 13.6 *Biological and Cultural Communications in the C-Space.*

researchable. Indeed, one could go even further and ask whether the learning implied by the knowledge cycle does not have its equivalent in physical and biological processes and whether, if so, these would not find expression in transactional strategies in some way akin to those that we have presented. For example, is the distinction drawn between the central and the autonomous nervous systems one that would justify an assignment of nervous impulses (transactions) to the left hand or right hand part of the C-space respectively?

It is when these *internal* communication processes fail to satisfy an organism's biological needs that it is forced to look to the outside environment and to *externalize* some of its transactions. Some of these externalizations are social and lead to the elaboration of social structure, some involve interaction with the physical world and lead to the creation of artefacts. In both cases, culture emerges as the natural complement to biological processes. A form of analysis that integrates both the structure and flow characteristics of information has potentially much to offer (Figure 13.6).

And as this little exploration of the information perspective beyond the corporate horizon indicates, the manager who decides to experiment with C-space analysis in his own firm or organization, should at least be aware that the bottom line lies somewhere beyond his balance sheet.

Reference

1. Williamson, O., *Markets and Hierarchies: Analysis and Antitrust Implications*, Glencoe: The Free Press, 1975.

Index

absorption 89–90, 92, 126–7, 148, 190, 242
acculturation 191
adaptation 152
adverse selection 71
ambiguity 27, 38–9, 54, 73, 94, 123
anthropology
  cultural 12, 19, 21, 58, 69, 108, 133
  managerial 19–20, 75
anti-trust laws 213–14
Apple 170
appropriability 142
attractiveness, technology and 136–9
audience
  competent 63–5, 78
  interested 65–6
authority relations 72, 100, 122, 160

base technologies 143–4
behaviourist theory 126, 243
Bell, Daniel 13, 232
Bernstein, Basil 74
biological processes 242–6
boards 121–23, 126
Boston Consulting Group 136
brain 39–40
Braudel, Fernand 11
broadcasting 49–50
bureaucracy 97–9, 102, 115, 119–20, 123–5, 129, 175, 179, 183, 187, 205, 207, 213, 216, 241–2
  Chinese 222–3, 229–30, 232–3
  and enterprise evolution 160–3

C-space see culture space
capital, 14, 236
  transactional 174–5

capitalism 217, 219–20
cellular communication 244
censorship 88, 92
centrifugal & centripetal firms 175–7, 232
Chandler, Alfred 153
channel 43, 164
charismatic authority 72–3, 100–2, 122, 241
China 20, 171, 196, 212, 218–33, 241
City of London 105–6
clan 102–4, 122–3, 125, 130, 162, 167, 175, 180, 187, 192, 195, 200, 214, 229, 239
classification, and coding 35–6
code
  choosing 26–8
  private & public 35
  restricted 74, 102
codification 54–5, 58, 127, 164, 242
  and internationalization 200–204
  in practice 114–18
  and problem solving 85–6
  and technology 135
  see also coding
codification-diffusion theory (C-D theory) 59–76, 140, 207, 235–7
codification scale 32–4, 36–9, 60–2, 115–16, 138, 187
coding
  and classification 35–6
  and codification 54–5
  communication as 25–6, 42
  and experience 35–6
  levels 30–2, 37–8, 62
  as mapping 34–5
  mastering 36–40

coding – *cont'd*.
  and memory 28
  as selection 30–2
  see also codification
collaboration 20, 150
collegial process 103
common sense 73–4, 76, 80, 102
communication
  and coding 25–9, 33–4, 42
  hierarchy 51–3
  model 42–4
  networks 47–9
  Shannon's problems 44–7, 62–3,
    65–6
  strategy 66–8, 75, 80–1, 93
  technology 154–5, 160, 163
communism 220–21, 229
competent audience 63–5, 78
competition 150
  competitive advantage 144, 155, 212
  competitive dynamics 147–8
  competitive phase 129
  technological 197–200
competitiveness 136–8, 170
complexity 11–12, 17, 104, 232
  product 189
computer 115, 164, 234
Confucianism 229
connotation 34
consensus 210–11
convergence 204–7
  and China 220–1
  and Japanese firm 207–11, 215–6
  reverse 215
co-ordination 155–8, 161
Copernicus 53
core competencies 135
corporate culture 20, 128, 131, 152–3,
    163, 167–8, 200, 202–17, 235,
    240–1
  centripetal v. centrifugal 175–7
cosmologies 104–5
costs
  of internationalization 191–5
  transaction 172–5, 182, 186–7,
    189–90, 195, 202
creativity 85
critical resources 107–8

CT-Scanner 150
cultural anthropology 12, 19, 21, 58,
    69, 108, 133
culture 12–13, 18, 21, 39–40, 68, 93,
    108, 133, 216, 219, 234, 238–9,
    246
  convergence theory 204, 206
  foreign 191–3, 195–6, 213
  national 20
  see also corporate culture
culture space (C-space) 67–8, 76, 235,
    237–9, 241
  corporate culture in 202–17
  entropy in 79–82
  external transactions in 169–84
  firm in 113–32, 152–68
  knowledge cycles in 81–2, 93
  multinationals in 185–201
  transactions in 104–5
  vectors in 77–9, 82

Darwin, Charles 89
data 84–5, 133, 165
  as factor of production 14–19
  see also information
  data processing 12, 14, 163–5
  decentralization 163, 229–31
  decoding 202–3
  delegation 98
  destination 43–4
  deviant perception 85, 92
  dichotomized scale 114
  diffusion 56, 58, 236, 242
  controlling 118, 183
  and knowledge cycle 86–8, 92, 126,
    149
  in practice 114–18
  scale 47, 49–54, 60–2, 91, 116, 138
  stretched 193, 200
  see also codification-diffusion theory
director responsibility system 224, 227
distributors 182–3, 189–91, 213
divisional structure 158–61
Douglas, Mary 104
downsizing 177
Drucker, Peter 13, 19
dynamics 75, 81–2
  competitive 147–8

economic development 204
economic rent 140–1, 144–5
economic theory *see* political economy
effectiveness problem 45–6, 62, 65, 67, 81
effort, least 64
emergent technologies 143–5
employment practices, Japanese 208–9
engineering firm 175, 182
enterprise *see* firm
entrepreneur 241
entropy 140–2
   in C-space 79–82, 197
esoteric strategies 67
Establishment 239
ethnocentric firm 194
evolution
   cultural 17
   industry 129–30
evolutionary production function 17–18, 242
experience
   and coding 27–30, 33–6
   shared 30, 33, 55–7
   structuring 28–9, 42, 85
   transmitting 55–7
exporting 189
external relations 169–84, 245
externalization 177
Exxon 242

face-to-face procedures 31, 49–50, 123, 173, 187, 189, 205, 210–11, 213
family firm 154, 157, 163, 184
feedback 49–50, 126–8, 242
Fermi, Enrico 100
feudal relationships 101–2, 205, 215–16, 223, 228–30
Fiat 194
fief 99–103, 118, 121–3, 129, 160, 162, 175, 187, 200, 205, 207, 241
   in China 223, 228–9, 231
   in Japan 213, 215–17
filtering 51
firm 20, 107
   centrifugal & centripetal 175–7
   evolution of 152–68
   external relations 169–84

in the C-space 113–32
Japanese 207–17
large 154–11, 177, 180, 208–10, 213
multinational 185–201, 207
small 169, 177, 181, 184, 208
subcultures 118–22
Fleming, Alexander 72
forgetting 79–81
functional firm 154, 158–9, 163

Galbraith, John Kenneth 204
Garratt, Bob 81
Geneen, Harold 162
General Electric 150
Genetech 150
geocentric firm 194
Georgescu-Roegen, N. 141
gestures *see* non-verbal communication
government, host 195–7
growth, organizational 128, 152–70, 184

Hamel, Gary, & Prahalad, C. K. 135
hardware 133, 135, 206
Heliocentric theory 53
Hewlett-Packard 167
hierarchy 180–81, 207, 228–9
   administrative 221–2
   of communication 51–3
   organizational 71, 98–9, 101, 121, 156, 158, 161–2, 170, 223
Hoffman la Roche 151
holding company (H-form) 158, 160, 162–3
Holton, Gerald 100
humour 30

IBM 162
idealism 105
ideology 232–3
impersonal transactions 57, 96, 98, 163, 173, 202, 205, 223
industrial corporation *see* firm
industry evolution 129–30
information 21, 108, 236
   exchange of 12–13, 18–19
   as factor of production 13–14, 106

information – *cont'd.*
  flows 77, 82, 92, 117, 152, 222, 237
  hoarding 148
  sharing of 42–58, 148
  structuring of 12–13, 18–19, 25–41
  and technology 135, 142
  as wealth 13–15, 236–7
  see also knowledge
information revolution 13, 18
information technology (IT) 164–7,
    200, 215
infrastructure
  communication 67, 227–8
  transactional 106, 174–6, 181–3,
    191, 195–6, 213
innovation, product 125–9, 175, 193
institutions 106–7, 181–3, 238–9
interested audience 65–6
internalization 170–2, 190
internationalization 20, 185–204, 206,
    212–13
intrapreneurship 168
investment 67, 227
  foreign 195–6, 212
  organizational 129, 156, 159
  prior 63–4, 88, 91, 106
ITT 162

Japan 13, 63, 196, 204–5, 219
  firm 20, 180–1, 194, 207–18, 240
  Ministry of International Trade &
    Industry 211
jargon 74, 102
Job, Steve 170
joint ventures 179–80, 191–2
Joyce, James: *Ulysses* 27
Just-in-Time manufacturing 143, 181

key technologies 143–5
Kluckhohn, Clyde 12
know-how 100, 134–5, 148, 183
knowledge 17–18, 240
  cycle 77–93, 107, 125–30, 143, 145,
    147–8, 175, 183, 190–3, 197–8,
    207, 238, 241–3, 245
  new 17, 81–4, 86–91, 93
  personal 29, 71–3, 76, 85, 100–1
  as power 52–4, 88, 94, 99

proprietary 70–1, 76, 80, 97, 127,
    178–9, 183
  protection of 87–8, 142–3, 183
  public 29, 69–70, 76, 95
  social 67, 75
  and technology 133, 140
  typology of 68–9, 75
  see also information
Kroeber, Alfred 12

labour 14
language 27, 30, 39, 45, 63, 186
  computer 164–5
large firm 154–61, 177, 180, 208, 213
learning 17, 81, 126, 148, 190, 192,
    242–3, 245
legal institutions 182, 196
Lewin, Kurt 113
licensing 178–9, 212

McLuhan, Marshall 65
Mafia 239–40
management 157
  Chinese 218–33
  dysfunctions 124
  of knowledge cycle 128
  Japanese 208–12, 215, 218
  socialization of 194
  styles 122–5, 153, 163, 169, 171–2,
    175
managerial anthropology 19–20, 75
mapping, coding as 34–5
market 95–7, 103–4, 114, 121, 123,
    129, 163, 171, 176–7, 183, 187,
    190, 200, 213, 215–16, 222, 231
  and convergence 205–7
  co-ordination through 158, 161–2
  horizontal 154
  integrated 155–6
Marx, Karl 107, 204, 216
materialism 105–7
meaning 47
memory 17, 28, 187
mobility of information 237–8
modernization 232
  in China 218–33
  in Japan 205–17, 217–20
monopolistic phase 129, 213

moral hazards 71
multidivisional structure (M-form) 158–61, 162–3
multinational firm 185–201, 207

national culture 20
negotiation 103
nervous system 244–5
networks, communication 47–9
Nissan 15, 139
noise 44, 46, 51, 62, 193
non-verbal communication 25–6, 50, 115

oligopolistic phase 130, 214
organization 12, 169
organizational
  assets 183
  capabilities 135
  growth 128, 152–70, 184
  mismatch 124–5
  structure 20, 114, 131
orgware 134–5
Ouchi, William 215
owner-manager 157, 160

paperwork 115
patented knowledge 87, 142–3, 179
Perlmutter, Howard 194
personal knowledge 29, 71–3, 76, 85, 100–1
personality 39
personalized transactions 100, 102, 166
planned economy 219–24, 226–7
Polanyi, Michael 29, 71–2
political economy of information 13, 21, 107–8, 234, 236–9
polycentric firm 194
Popper, Karl 60
portfolio, technology 135–40, 142–3
power
  knowledge as 52–4, 88, 94, 99
  personal 72–3, 100–1, 103
Prahalad, C. K., *see* Hamel, Gary
printed matter 60, 69–70
prior
  investment 63–4, 88, 91, 106
  knowledge 46, 55–6, 63, 77, 102

private
  codes 34–5
  knowledge 29–30
problem 83–4
problem solving 85–6, 92, 126, 148
product
  complexity 189
  divisions 158–9
product-market portfolio 136–8, 140, 142
production 129, 156, 222
  department 118–20, 122–4, 126, 179
  factors of 13–19, 106
  function 14, 17–18
professional transactions 102–3
proprietary knowledge 70–1, 76, 80, 97, 129, 178–9, 183
proselytizing strategies 67
protection of knowledge 87–8
public
  codes 35
  knowledge 29, 69–70, 76, 96

quasi-firm 174

radio 49–50
real estate 184
receiver 43
recruitment 31–2, 209
redundancy 44–5, 54, 62, 73, 202
regiocentric firm 194
relay 47, 49, 51, 126
research & development 99–101, 107, 122–3, 125–6, 197–9
  in C-space 118–19
research firm 175, 181–2, 184
restricted code 74, 102
revolutions, technological 17–18, 154–5, 160

sales department 120, 122–6, 189–90
scale, economies of 143, 155–6
scanning 50–2, 83–5, 91–2, 99, 122, 126, 149, 183, 192–3, 195, 242
scarcity 140, 142
scope of the firm 20, 166
selection
  adverse 71
  coding as 30–2, 37, 85

semantic
  noise 46
  problem 45–6, 63, 67, 81
Shannon, Claude, & Weaver, Warren
  communication problems 44–7,
    62–3, 65–7, 166
sharing
  of experience 30, 33, 55–7, 72
  of information 12–13, 18–19, 42–58
  of values 55–6, 67, 73, 100–2,
    121–2, 173, 180–2, 191
sign systems, as coding 28, 34
skills 134, 210
small firm 169, 177, 181, 184, 208
social
  knowledge 67, 75
  relationships 95
socialism 219, 232
socialization 73, 194
software 133–5
source 42
Stalk, G., Evans, P., & Shulman, L.
  135
start-up phase 129, 241
Stimulus-Response 126, 128, 242
strategic ethnocentrism 193
strategy 235
  communication 66–8, 75, 80–1
  transactional 94–108
structuring
  of data 12–13, 19, 25–41
  of experience 28–9, 42, 85
sub-contracting 180–91, 209, 211
subcultures, enterprise 118–23, 231
  integrating 125–9
subjective knowledge 72
symbols, as coding 28, 32, 34, 38
system, technology as 139–40, 146

tapered integration 172
target audience 66–7
technical problem 44–6, 67, 81
technology 13–14, 20, 63, 130–31,
    133–51, 169, 206, 212, 216, 235
  competition in 197–200
  and evolution of firm 154–5, 162–4
  new 128–9, 135–6, 155–6
  transfer 199–200

telecommunications 165, 203–4
Third World 218
Thorn-EMI 150
3M 168
trading 175, 177–8, 181
training 210
transactional
  costs 172–5, 182, 186–7, 189–90,
    195, 202
  infrastructures 106, 174–6, 181–3,
    191, 195–6, 213
  strategies 94–108
transmitter 42–3
transmitting experience 55–7
trust 56–7, 73, 100–1, 103, 123, 181,
    191
typology of knowledge 68–9, 75

uncodified
  communication 54–8, 94
  information 121, 192
United States
  corporate culture 213–15
  large firms 154–8, 213
  multinationals 207
utility
  creating 140–41
  of information 236

value
  of information 236–7
  paradox of 140–8
  of new knowledge 87
values 133
  shared 55–6, 67, 73, 100–2, 121–2,
    173, 180–2, 191
vectors in C-space 77–9, 82
vision, singular 85
Volkswagen 196

Walras, Leon 140
wars of movement & position 143–6,
    184
wealth, information as 13–15, 236–7
Weaver, Warren *see* Shannon, Claude
Weber, Max 102, 222–3
Williamson, Oliver 237
Wittgenstein, L. 25

What is AMED?

AMED is an association of individuals who have a professional interest in the development of people at work. Our membership is exclusive to individuals. AMED's network brings together people from industry, the public sector, academic organizations and consultancy.

The aims of the association

- to promote best practice in the fields of individual and organizational development

- to provide a forum for exploration of new ideas

- to provide our members with opportunities for their own development

- to encourage the adoption of ethical practices

Benefits of membership

- an extensive network of contacts

- regional groups spanning the UK and Europe

- shared experience of working on leading-edge issues

- local meetings and special interest networking activities

- a programme of national conferences, workshops and seminars

- a regular AMED newsletter and a quarterly journal

- a membership list and consultants' directory

- discounts on publications and professional insurances

- a national voice on development issues

Registered office:
Association for Management Education & Development
21 Catherine Street
London WC2B 5JS
Tel: 071 497 3264   Registered Charity No 269 706